P9-BYW-002

P9-BYW-002

EYEWITNESS
ELEMENTS

Written by
ADRIAN DINGLE

Stalactites made
of deposits of
calcium carbonate

Flakes of pure
gold refined in
a laboratory

DK | Penguin Random House

DK Delhi

Senior editor Rupa Rao
Project art editor Pooja Pipil
Editor Charvi Arora
Art editors Mansi Agrawal, Priyanka Bansal
Jacket designer Juhi Sheth
Jackets editorial coordinator Priyanka Sharma
Senior DTP designer Harish Aggarwal
DTP designers Pawan Kumar,
Syed Md Farhan, Vikram Singh
Managing jackets editor Saloni Singh
Pre-production manager Balwant Singh
Production manager Pankaj Sharma
Managing editor Kingshuk Ghoshal
Managing art editor Govind Mittal

DK London

Senior editor Ashwin Khurana
Senior art editor Spencer Holbrook
Picture researcher Liz Moore
US Editor Jill Hamilton
US Executive editor Lori Cates Hand
Jacket designer Surabhi Wadhwa-Gandhi
Jacket editor Claire Gell
Jacket design development manager Sophia MTT
Producer, pre-production Andy Hilliard
Senior producer Angela Graef
Managing editor Francesca Baines
Managing art editor Philip Letsu
Publisher Andrew Macintyre
Associate publishing director Liz Wheeler
Art director Karen Self
Design director Phil Ormerod
Publishing director Jonathan Metcalf

Written by Adrian Dingle
Consultant: John Gillespie, M. Sc.

First American Edition, 2018
Published in the United States by DK Publishing
345 Hudson Street, New York, New York 10014

Copyright © 2018 Dorling Kindersley Limited
DK, a division of Penguin Random House LLC
18 19 20 21 22 10 9 8 7 6 5 4 3 2 1
001–310003–June/2018

A catalog record for this book
is available from the Library of Congress.
ISBN: 978-1-4654-7404-9 (PLC)
ISBN: 978-1-4654-7405-6 (ALB)

DK books are available at special discounts when
purchased in bulk for sales promotions, premiums,
fund-raising, or educational use. For details, contact:
DK Publishing Special Markets, 345 Hudson Street,
New York, New York 10014
SpecialSales@dk.com

Printed and bound in China

A WORLD OF IDEAS:
SEE ALL THERE IS TO KNOW

www.dk.com

Pure iodine stored
in a glass sphere

The Eiffel
Tower, Paris,
France, made
of wrought iron

Copper wire

**Pure mercury at
room temperature**

Contents

What is an element?

An element is a substance that cannot be broken down into simpler ingredients. Each one is made up of building blocks called atoms, which are unique for every element. For example, the element carbon contains only carbon atoms. There are 118 elements, and most are found naturally on Earth, such as oxygen and gold. Elements are vital to our everyday lives, whether it is calcium keeping our bones strong or hydrogen powering environmentally friendly buses.

French chemist
Antoine Lavoisier

Early ideas
The ancient Greeks believed the world was made of just four elements—earth, water, fire, and air. In medieval times, the study of the elements was a mixture of science and magic. Alchemists searched in vain for the Philosopher's Stone, a material they believed could turn metals such as lead into gold. The first breakthroughs in chemistry came in the 1700s. One important early chemist was Antoine Lavoisier, who showed that sulfur was an element, and water was not an element but a compound of hydrogen and oxygen.

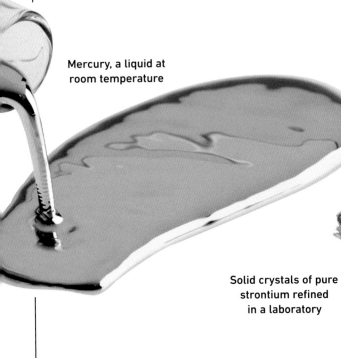

Mercury, a liquid at
room temperature

Solid crystals of pure
strontium refined
in a laboratory

Elemental forms
All of the elements exist in one of three primary states under normal conditions of temperature and pressure: they are a solid, a liquid, or a gas, although a fourth special state called plasma is sometimes seen. Most elements are solids, except a few that are gases. Only mercury and bromine exist as liquids at room temperature.

States of matter

Elements can exist in three states: solid, liquid, and gas. An element can change from one state to another. For example, solid gallium can melt into a liquid, while liquid bromine can evaporate into a gas. The changes do not alter the atoms of the element, but arrange them in a more, or less, rigid way.

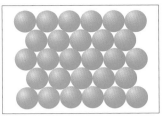

Solid
In solids, the atoms are attracted to one another, are arranged in a regular pattern, and have little energy to move around.

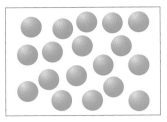

Liquid
As solids become liquids, the attraction between the atoms weakens. They have no fixed arrangement and more energy.

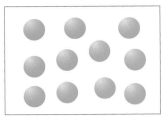

Gas
As liquids become gases, the atoms are only very weakly attracted to each other. They spread out as far as possible, and have a lot of energy.

Raw forms

Elements are commonly found in one of two ways. If they are unreactive and do not easily combine with other elements, they may be found in their pure state, such as gold. Elements that are more reactive always combine with the other elements around them. This combination of elements is called a compound. Compounds occur naturally and need to be extracted through a chemical process.

Gold in quartz

Compounds

When elements chemically bond with one another in a fixed ratio, they form compounds. For example, in sodium chloride, sodium combines with chlorine in an equal ratio to form a compound. Water is a compound that forms from two hydrogen atoms combining with one atom of oxygen to produce one molecule.

Common salt
(sodium chloride)

Mixtures

When elements or compounds combine in an unequal ratio without chemically bonding with one another, the resulting combination is called a mixture. For example, any combination of salt and sand contains two separate things, not chemically bonded to one another, and in no particular fixed quantities. Seen to the right is a mixture of soap foam and food coloring, which can be separated by filtering.

Pure hydrogen gas in a glass sphere

The human body

About 99 percent of the human body is made from just six elements: oxygen, carbon, hydrogen, nitrogen, calcium, and phosphorus. They combine to form thousands of different compounds. More than 60 percent of the body is water, but a total of 25 elements are required to make our body work properly. They are called the "essential elements."

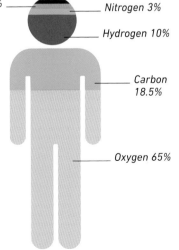

Phosphorus 1%

Others 1%

Calcium 1.5%

Nitrogen 3%

Hydrogen 10%

Carbon 18.5%

Oxygen 65%

Inside an atom

Everything in the Universe is made of very small particles called atoms. Atoms are so tiny that they cannot be seen with the naked eye. They are the smallest units of any element, but the atoms themselves are made up of even smaller "subatomic" particles called protons, electrons, and neutrons. The number of protons in an atom of an element is unique to that element.

Electrons travel around the nucleus in three-dimensional areas of space called orbitals.

The dense nucleus at the center of the atom is where nearly all the mass of an atom lies.

Subatomic particles
Protons and neutrons are found in the core, or nucleus, at the center of the atom, while electrons orbit the nucleus. Protons and electrons have exactly equal but opposite charges; protons are positive, and electrons are negative. Neutrons carry no charge. Because atoms have an equal number of protons and electrons, and neutrons contribute no charge, atoms in their natural state are neutral. Protons and neutrons have the same mass while electrons are about 10,000 times smaller.

The orbitals are arranged around the nucleus, at various distances, in layers called shells.

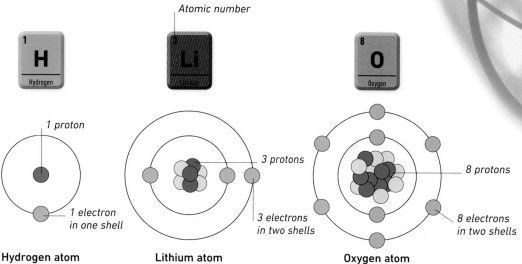

Atomic number

1	**3**	**8**
H	Li	O
Hydrogen	Lithium	Oxygen

1 proton

1 electron in one shell

3 protons

3 electrons in two shells

8 protons

8 electrons in two shells

Hydrogen atom   **Lithium atom**   **Oxygen atom**

What is the atomic number?
The atomic number of an element tells us how many protons are found inside the nucleus of a single atom of that element. For example, a lithium atom (above) has three protons in its nucleus, which means its atomic number is 3. The elements are arranged on the periodic table in the increasing order of their atomic number, starting with hydrogen, the simplest element with just one proton.

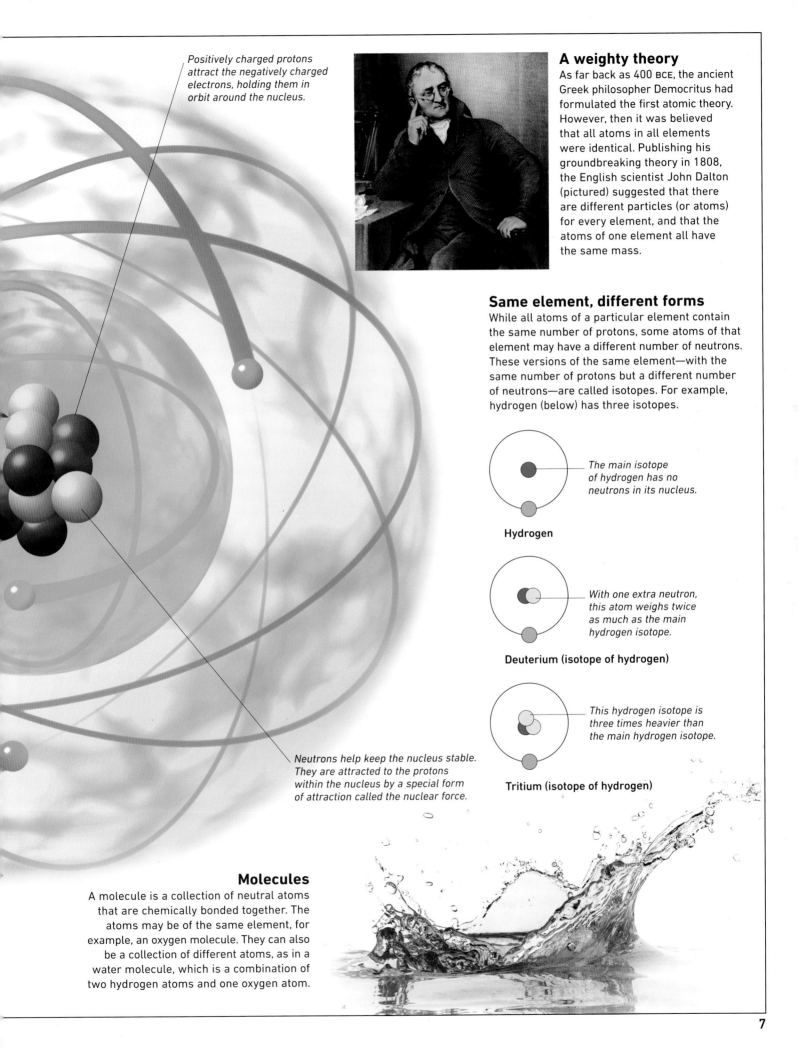

Positively charged protons attract the negatively charged electrons, holding them in orbit around the nucleus.

A weighty theory

As far back as 400 BCE, the ancient Greek philosopher Democritus had formulated the first atomic theory. However, then it was believed that all atoms in all elements were identical. Publishing his groundbreaking theory in 1808, the English scientist John Dalton (pictured) suggested that there are different particles (or atoms) for every element, and that the atoms of one element all have the same mass.

Same element, different forms

While all atoms of a particular element contain the same number of protons, some atoms of that element may have a different number of neutrons. These versions of the same element—with the same number of protons but a different number of neutrons—are called isotopes. For example, hydrogen (below) has three isotopes.

The main isotope of hydrogen has no neutrons in its nucleus.

Hydrogen

With one extra neutron, this atom weighs twice as much as the main hydrogen isotope.

Deuterium (isotope of hydrogen)

This hydrogen isotope is three times heavier than the main hydrogen isotope.

Tritium (isotope of hydrogen)

Neutrons help keep the nucleus stable. They are attracted to the protons within the nucleus by a special form of attraction called the nuclear force.

Molecules

A molecule is a collection of neutral atoms that are chemically bonded together. The atoms may be of the same element, for example, an oxygen molecule. They can also be a collection of different atoms, as in a water molecule, which is a combination of two hydrogen atoms and one oxygen atom.

The periodic table

Many scientists had tried to arrange the known elements into an organized list long before the Russian chemist Dmitri Mendeleev produced his first table of elements in 1869. Mendeleev's table was periodic, or repeating, because the characteristics of elements followed a pattern. It was the forerunner to the modern periodic table.

Reading the table

The periodic table is made up of a series of groups (columns that run from top to bottom), and periods (rows that run from left to right).

Groups
Elements in the same group have the same number of electrons in their outermost shell. As you move down a group, the atoms of the elements get larger and heavier. This is because there are an increasing number of protons in the nucleus, and more electrons arranged in shells surrounding the nucleus.

One shell

Hydrogen
An atom of hydrogen has one electron.

Two shells

Lithium
A lithium atom has three electrons, with one in its outer shell.

Three shells

Sodium
A sodium atom has eleven electrons, with one in its outer shell.

Groups
A vertical column of chemically similar elements is known as a group.

Periods
A horizontal row of chemically different elements is known as a period.

KEY

- Hydrogen
- Alkali Metals
- Alkaline Earth Metals
- Transition Metals
- Lanthanides
- Actinides
- The Boron Group
- The Carbon Group
- The Nitrogen Group
- The Oxygen Group
- Halogens
- Noble Gases

Lanthanides and actinides
The "f" block elements are sometimes called the inner transition metals.

Groups (columns)

Periods (rows)

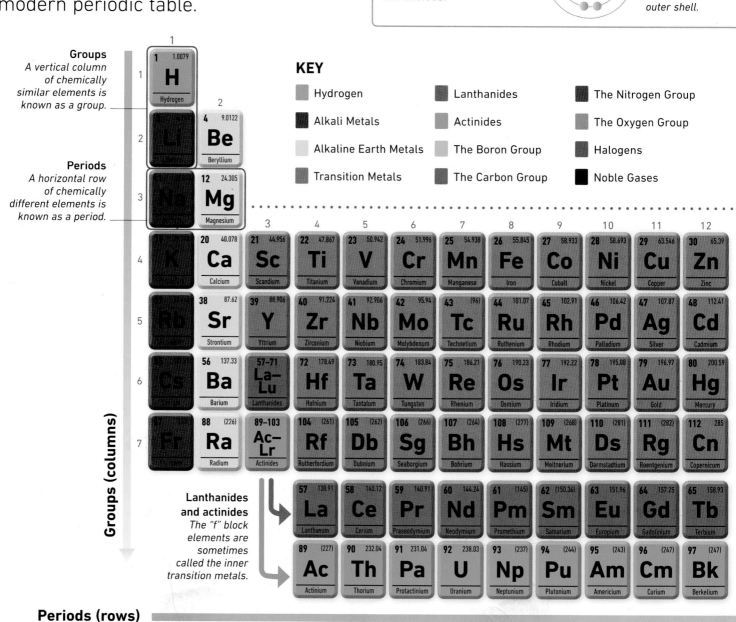

Periods

As you move across a period, the atoms of each element have the same number of shells. However, as you move across the period the number of electrons in the outer shell increases. In the examples below, each element has three shells. The different numbers of electrons in the outer shells mean that these elements have differences in their chemical properties.

 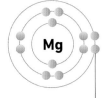 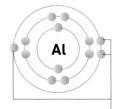

| *One electron* | *Two electrons* | *Three electrons* |

Sodium
A sodium atom has eleven electrons in total, with one in its outer shell.

Magnesium
A magnesium atom has twelve electrons in total, with two in its outer shell.

Aluminum
An aluminum atom has thirteen electrons in total, with three in its outer shell.

Blocks

Within the periodic table there are larger collections of elements known as blocks. Three of these blocks—the "s" block, the "d" block, and the "f" block—contain elements that have many broad similarities with one another, but the "p" block contains a much more diverse set of elements.

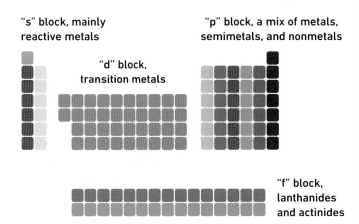

"s" block, mainly reactive metals

"d" block, transition metals

"p" block, a mix of metals, semimetals, and nonmetals

"f" block, lanthanides and actinides

Elemental information

Each element is given a tile with important information to identify it. These include the element's name, symbol, atomic number, and atomic mass number.

Atomic number
This is the number of protons in the nucleus of an atom of an element. A beryllium atom has four protons in its nucleus, so its atomic number is four.

Atomic mass number
This number shows the average mass of the atoms of all the naturally occurring forms (isotopes) of a given element. Beryllium has 12 known isotopes, and their average mass is 9.0122 AMU (atomic mass units).

4 9.0122
Be
Beryllium

Name
The elements are named after people, places, their sources, and many other things.

Chemical symbol
Each element is given a one- or two-letter symbol. This is the shortened version of the element's English or Latin name. The first letter is always uppercase, and where there are two letters, the second is always lowercase.

Dmitri Mendeleev

The Russian scientist Mendeleev is usually thought of as the "father" of the modern periodic table. His original arrangement organized the elements by atomic mass, and also left gaps that accurately predicted the existence of some unknown elements, which would be discovered later.

Elemental groups and sets

Within the periodic table, elements are divided into smaller groups and sets that often have similar chemical properties, or are related to one another in some other way.

Hydrogen

As the most abundant element in the Universe, hydrogen is unique. While it is placed at the top of the alkali metals on the periodic table, hydrogen is a gas, and it behaves nothing like those metals.

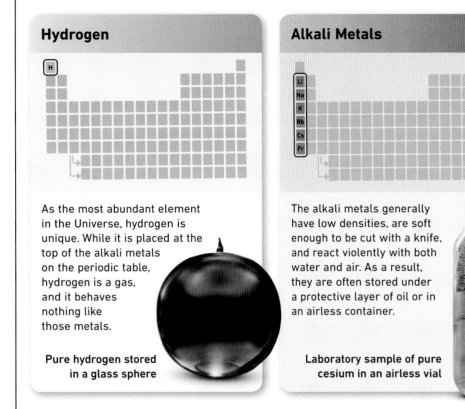

Pure hydrogen stored in a glass sphere

Alkali Metals

The alkali metals generally have low densities, are soft enough to be cut with a knife, and react violently with both water and air. As a result, they are often stored under a protective layer of oil or in an airless container.

Laboratory sample of pure cesium in an airless vial

Alkaline Earth Metals

A little less reactive than their group 1 neighbors, the alkaline earth metals get their name from the fact that most of them were discovered in the form of their oxide compounds, in the earth.

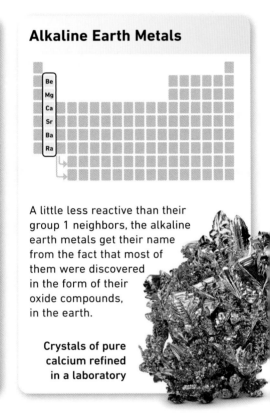

Crystals of pure calcium refined in a laboratory

Transition Metals

These metals form the largest set of elements in the periodic table. They share many properties with each other, such as their ability to form colored compounds, and are often used in specialized alloys.

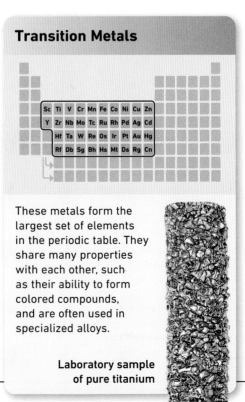

Laboratory sample of pure titanium

Lanthanides

Although they were once known as the "rare earths," the elements in this set are not rare at all. The idea of rarity came from the fact that they are difficult to separate from one another, so they proved to be difficult to find.

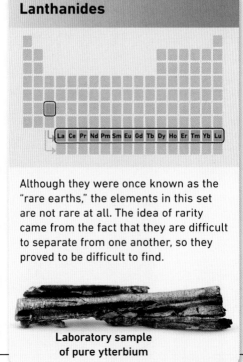

Laboratory sample of pure ytterbium

Actinides

A set of elements that are generally very radioactive, the actinides are not found commonly in nature, with a few exceptions. Many of them are only produced artificially, and have little use beyond research.

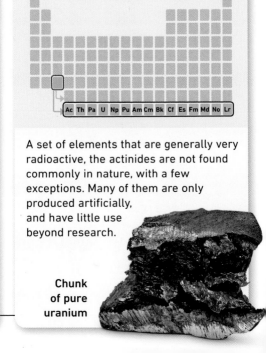

Chunk of pure uranium

The Boron Group

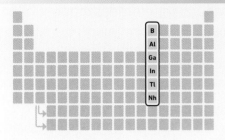

Although these elements are all not very reactive, they do differ in other ways. Aluminum has many uses, including in construction; gallium is a liquid metal, and thallium is poisonous.

Pellets of pure aluminum refined in a laboratory

The Carbon Group

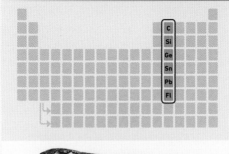

Laboratory sample of pure tin

Group 14 includes the nonmetal carbon, the semimetals silicon and germanium, the metals tin and lead, and the radioactive element flerovium—the newest member of the group.

The Nitrogen Group

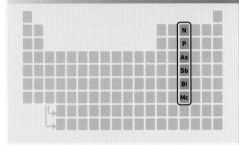

Nonmetals, semimetals, and metals make up the nitrogen group. Members of this group include a gas, some solids, and moscovium—an artificial element that is not yet well understood.

Bismuth crystals refined in a laboratory

The Oxygen Group

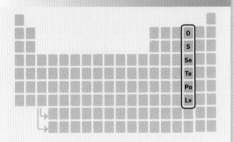

The elements in group 16 are diverse. There are two nonmetals (oxygen and sulfur), three semimetals (selenium, tellurium, and polonium), and livermorium, which remains mysterious because it is a relatively new element.

Chunk of pure selenium refined in a laboratory

Halogens

The word "halogen" means "salt forming." This comes from the fact that the group 17 elements will readily form salts when combined with metals. For instance, iodine reacts with potassium to form a salt called potassium iodide.

Pure bromine stored in a glass sphere

Noble Gases

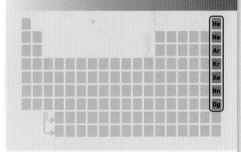

Colorless, odorless, and tasteless, the group 18 elements are not very reactive at all. Their tendency to not mix with the other elements led to them being called "noble," in the same way that a king or queen does not mix with common folk.

Pure argon stored in a glass sphere

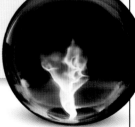

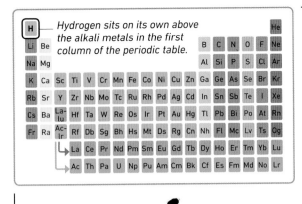

Hydrogen sits on its own above the alkali metals in the first column of the periodic table.

Hydrogen

1 H

The first member of the periodic table, hydrogen is the simplest and lightest of all the elements. Although it is the most abundant element in the Universe, you cannot smell, taste, or see hydrogen. It is a gas found in stars and planets. Large planets, such as Jupiter, have atmospheres made of hydrogen mixed with other gases. On Earth, hydrogen has many uses, from drinking water to environmentally sustainable fuel.

Pure hydrogen gas is stored inside this glass sphere, and gives off a purple glow when electrified.

The Orion Nebula also contains elements such as iron, silicon, carbon, oxygen, and helium.

Clouds in space

Hydrogen is abundant in the Orion Nebula, which is a dense cloud of hot gases and dust in space. Within these clouds of gas, new stars are born when hydrogen and other gases contract under the pressure of gravity. This nebula is located 1,500 light-years away from Earth, meaning it takes 1,500 years for light to reach us from this cosmic cloud.

Life-giver

Water is vital to life on Earth. A single molecule of water contains two atoms of hydrogen and one atom of oxygen. Earth's surface is 71 percent water, in the form of oceans and lakes, which is where most of the world's hydrogen is found.

Powering the Sun

The Sun is a massive ball of flaming hydrogen and helium. The source of the Sun's energy is its hot, dense core, where hydrogen atoms undergo a process of fusion to produce the gas helium. More than 600 tons of hydrogen is converted into helium each second, releasing intense heat and light.

The Sun is about 75 percent hydrogen.

1. This chamber contains liquid hydrogen.

2. This chamber contains liquid oxygen.

3. Pumps control the flow of the liquids as they enter the combustion chamber.

4. The combustion chamber is where the liquids come together, creating an explosive mixture that is ignited to create hot steam.

5. Explosive mixture passes through the nozzle, creating steam that pushes the rocket upward.

Rocket fuel

Modern space rockets are powered by liquid hydrogen. This element combines with liquid oxygen to create extremely hot steam, which escapes out of the nozzle with great force. This produces a thrust that pushes the rocket upward. As an added benefit, this process generates only steam as a by-product, making hydrogen an environmentally safe choice of fuel.

Fritz Haber on a German postage stamp

Making ammonia

The combination of hydrogen and nitrogen produces ammonia, a vital compound in fertilizers that aids plant growth. Known as the Haber Process, this technique was developed by the German chemist Fritz Haber in the early 20th century and is still widely used today.

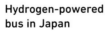

Hydrogen-powered bus in Japan

Hindenburg disaster

In 1936, the German airship *Hindenburg* was the biggest aircraft ever built. It was filled with hydrogen, which easily catches fire and burns with an extremely hot flame. In 1937, the *Hindenburg* caught fire due to a stray spark that ignited leaking hydrogen gas. The accident killed 36 people.

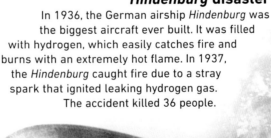

Clean fuel

Pure hydrogen is a clean energy source and is used to power some vehicles, such as this bus. When hydrogen is passed through a fuel cell (a type of battery that needs to be continually filled up), it chemically fuses with oxygen from the air. This reaction can be used to produce electricity, which powers the motor inside the vehicle.

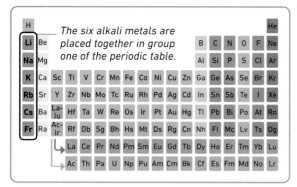

The six alkali metals are placed together in group one of the periodic table.

Alkali Metals

Sitting below hydrogen on the periodic table are the alkali metals. A group of six similar elements, these metals react vigorously with water to produce hydrogen gas and alkaline solutions (solutions containing reactive chemicals called alkalis), and with the oxygen in air to produce compounds called oxides. Alkali metals are highly reactive and are not found in their pure form in nature, but as compounds. Pure alkali metals are shiny, and soft enough to be cut with a knife.

Lithium

Li 3

Pure lithium is so light that it can float on water. However, if left in the open, this silvery metal can tarnish in minutes. To prevent this from happening, it has to be stored in mineral oil. Discovered in 1817, lithium has a wide range of commercial uses today. For instance, it is mixed with magnesium and aluminum to form lightweight alloys used to manufacture some aircraft and trains. It is a key element in rechargeable batteries. Lithium is also useful in medicines.

This pure alkali metal turns dull when exposed to air.

Laboratory-refined piece of pure lithium

In nature
An important source of lithium is lepidolite. This violet-pink mineral gets its name from two Greek words, *lepidos*, which means "scales," and *lithos*, meaning "stone." It is so named because lepidolite often grows scalelike plates.

Soaking it up
Minerals containing lithium dissolve easily in water. Seas and oceans throughout the world are filled with vast amounts of lithium. As a result, sea creatures, such as the common lobster, are rich in lithium, which they absorb from seawater.

Powerful battery
Rechargeable lithium-ion batteries are widely used in modern electronic devices, such as smartphones. Not only are they lightweight and small, these batteries also allow people to use their mobile phones for a long time between charges.

Sodium

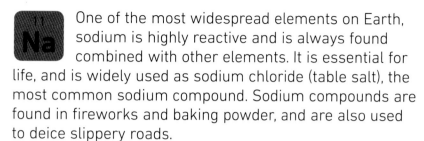 One of the most widespread elements on Earth, sodium is highly reactive and is always found combined with other elements. It is essential for life, and is widely used as sodium chloride (table salt), the most common sodium compound. Sodium compounds are found in fireworks and baking powder, and are also used to deice slippery roads.

Transparent, cube-shaped crystal

Halite

A mineral called halite contains sodium chloride. More commonly known as rock salt, this compound is vital for human and animal health. Halite is found as cubic crystals, and forms as deposits around seas and lakes in dry climates when the saltwater evaporates.

Dead bodies were dried using natron.

Preserved forever

Uses for sodium go all the way back to ancient Egypt. The Egyptians believed in an afterlife, so they preserved the dead in a process called mummification. They used a mixture called natron—a combination of different sodium compounds—to absorb the water in the body to dry it out before wrapping it in linen.

Pure sodium in an airless vial

Baking powder

Sodium hydrogen carbonate—better known as baking powder—is added to cake batter in baking. When mixed with acidic ingredients, the baking powder releases carbon dioxide gas, which helps the batter rise, giving the cake a light, airy texture.

Heap of sea salt in a salt farm

Harvesting salt

Salt forms in some rocks and, over time, it dissolves and runs into seawater. In shallow pools, the wind and Sun quickly evaporate the water, leaving thick heaps of salt that can be collected by farmers.

Soft metal

Potassium is a soft metal that can be cut with a knife. This shiny, silvery metal tarnishes quickly when it reacts with oxygen in the air. This reaction forms a dull layer on the metal's surface. Cutting the metal again reveals the shiny surface once more.

Layer of a compound called potassium oxide

Potassium

With its low density, potassium is a typical group one metal. Like all alkali metals, potassium has the ability to react with cold water to form flammable hydrogen gas. As well as being an ingredient in many industrial products, such as fertilizers, potassium plays a key role in regulating our muscular and nervous systems and is important in our diet.

Banana

Potassium-rich foods

Celery

Coconut

Potassium in food

Various foods contain potassium. Bananas are often considered to be potassium-rich, but many other foods have higher percentages of this element. A cup of coconut water, for example, has 0.02 oz (600 mg) of potassium compared to 0.015 oz (422 mg) in a medium-sized banana. This useful element keeps the brain, nerves, and muscles functioning normally.

Sylvite

A naturally occurring mineral of potassium, sylvite is composed mainly of the compound potassium chloride. Sylvite is similar to halite, which is also known as sodium chloride or simply "salt."

Pink match head contains phosphorus and potassium chlorate

Explosive quality

Potassium chlorate, a compound of potassium, chlorine, and oxygen, is used in the manufacture of matches. When a match is struck, phosphorus and potassium chlorate mix in small amounts, and then ignite due to friction.

Plant food

Potassium is an essential element for plant growth. Its compounds are used extensively in fertilizers, along with phosphorus and nitrogen. In fact, fertilizers are often referred to by their "NPK" (nitrogen, phosphorous, potassium) content.

Potassium-based fertilizer sprayed on a field

Rubidium

From *rubidius*, which is Latin for "deep red," rubidium produces a red-colored flame when burned. Discovered by the German chemists Gustav Kirchhoff and Robert Bunsen in 1861, it has a low melting point of 102.2°F (39°C).

Pure rubidium is contained in this glass to prevent it from coming into contact with air and undergoing a violent reaction.

Laboratory sample of pure rubidium in an airless vial

Fireworks

Like many other group one elements, rubidium compounds can produce vivid colors when heated. For example, rubidium nitrate is sometimes used in fireworks to give a distinct purple color. It is also an ingredient in illumination flares used by the military to aid rescues and at sea as distress signals.

Cesium

Like other alkali metals, cesium must be stored away from water and air to avoid a violent reaction. An important application of cesium is in making atomic clocks—accurate timekeeping devices that can measure time down to a nanosecond (one thousand-millionth of a second).

Shiny, silver-gold metal

Laboratory sample of pure cesium in an airless vial

Solar cells

Adding cesium to a solar cell boosts the conductivity of silicon in the glass, increasing the cell's efficiency. Solar cells have a wide range of applications, from powering satellites in space to generating electricity on Earth.

Cesium-coated solar cell

Francium

This is one of the rarest elements on Earth, with only a few grams estimated to exist in the planet's crust. Because of this scarcity, francium was one of the last elements discovered, in 1939, by the physicist Marguerite Perey. It was named after her native country—France.

Uraninite

This mineral contains tiny amounts of francium, a result of the atoms of other elements in the ore undergoing radioactive decay.

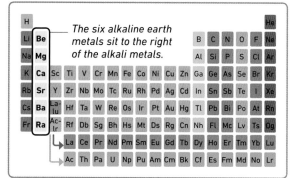
The six alkaline earth metals sit to the right of the alkali metals.

Alkaline Earth Metals

A slightly less reactive bunch than their group one neighbors, the group two elements are called "alkaline" because they form alkaline solutions on reacting with water. Soft and shiny when pure, they are solid at room temperature. First purified in the 19th century, they are called "earth metals" because many of them were discovered in their raw form in Earth's crust. Each element in this group burns with a distinctive color.

Beryllium

4 Be

Once called "glaucinium," meaning "sweet" (because of the sweet-tasting compounds made of this element), beryllium was eventually named after the mineral beryl. A toxic and radioactive element, beryllium can be a health hazard. This metal has many applications when alloyed with other elements, including its use in making missiles and satellites.

Aquamarine raw crystal

Aquamarine

One of the chief sources of beryllium is beryl, a naturally occurring mineral made from beryllium, aluminum, silicon, and oxygen. Beryl can take on many different colors depending on the impurities present. Aquamarine is a type of blue beryl gemstone: the presence of iron makes it blue.

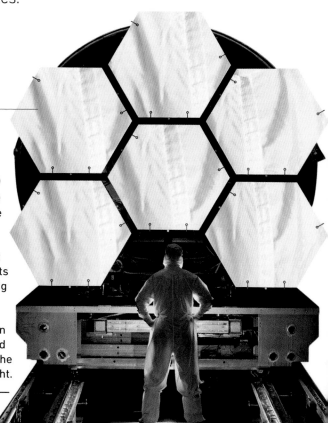

A single hexagonal mirror measures about 4½ ft (1.3 m) in diameter.

James Webb Space Telescope

NASA's James Webb Space Telescope is an Earth-orbiting telescope set for launch in 2019. It will be used to observe the Universe and to collect data about our Solar System, planets around other stars, and even the Big Bang—the event that gave birth to the Universe. Light from distant parts of space will be collected by an array of mirrors made of gold-plated beryllium. This element makes the mirrors strong and lightweight.

Magnesium

12 Mg This light metal is very reactive, including with oxygen in the air. When it burns, it produces a bright white glow that is so intense it can damage the eyes of anyone looking directly at the burning metal. Magnesium is used in flares and fireworks.

Yellowing leaves are a sign of magnesium deficiency.

Translucent, crystalline form

Shiny gray crystals

Laboratory sample of pure magnesium

Brittle mineral

Magnesite
This magnesium mineral is a good source of the compound magnesium oxide, which can be used as a material for lining furnaces because of its very high melting point and resistance to heat.

Chlorophyll
A green-colored compound found in leaves, chlorophyll converts sunlight into the energy that plants need for growth. This process is called photosynthesis. At the center of each chlorophyll molecule is a magnesium atom. Without magnesium, plants would not be able to carry out photosynthesis.

Medication cup helps measure the required dosage

Stomach settler
Magnesium carbonate is a common ingredient in medication used to ease heartburn and other stomach ailments. The carbonate reacts with excess acid in the stomach, turning it into water and releasing carbon dioxide gas in the process. This gas can also make you burp.

Finding magnesium
In 1755, the Scottish physician and chemist Joseph Black experimented on a compound called magnesium carbonate that led him to recognize magnesium as an element. In the same set of experiments, Black also identified the gas carbon dioxide.

These car rims are made of a magnesium–aluminum alloy for high strength and quality.

Custom-made car rims

Magnesium alloys
Alloys containing magnesium have the advantage of being both strong and lightweight. For that reason, several of them are used in the manufacture of high-performance machinery. One such alloy is called Mag–Thor: a mixture of magnesium, thorium, and other elements, it is used to build aircraft engines.

Calcium caves

In caves, deposits of the compound calcium carbonate (also known as limestone) form structures called stalactites and stalagmites. Stalactites hang from the roof, while stalagmites, which are composed of droppings from the ceiling of the cave, appear to grow up from the ground.

Stalactites take thousands of years to grow.

Calcium

Pure calcium is soft enough to cut with a knife.

20 Ca This soft, silver-white metal is the fifth most abundant element in Earth's crust. It strengthens bones in our body, and is essential for growth. Calcium compounds are also useful in industry and in construction. Calcium oxide, for example, is used in the production of cement. The compound calcium hydroxide is used by the paper industry and for treating sewage.

Acid controller

Calcium compounds are used to reduce acidity in various ways. For example, calcium supplements boost the growth of some plants by making the soil less acidic. Calcium compounds are also an ingredient in tablets that reduce acid-related discomfort in the stomach.

Indigestion tablets

Crystals of pure calcium refined in a laboratory

Producing iron

Calcium carbonate (limestone) is important in the production of pure iron. It is added to the raw materials in a blast furnace where it removes sand and other impurities from the iron ore. The mixture of the impurities and limestone, known as "slag," is then separated from the pure metal.

1. A mixture of raw materials, including calcium carbonate (limestone), is added to the furnace through this valve.

2. Hot air enters the furnace, heating up the materials inside.

3. Limestone mixes with sand and stones in the ore to form slag. This slag floats above the molten iron, and is collected from the furnace.

4. Pure molten iron sinks to the bottom, and it is then drained from the furnace.

Teeth and bones

Calcium is the most abundant metal in our body. Calcium compounds are responsible for the structure of human teeth and bones. We get calcium in our diet by eating calcium-rich food, including dairy products and nuts.

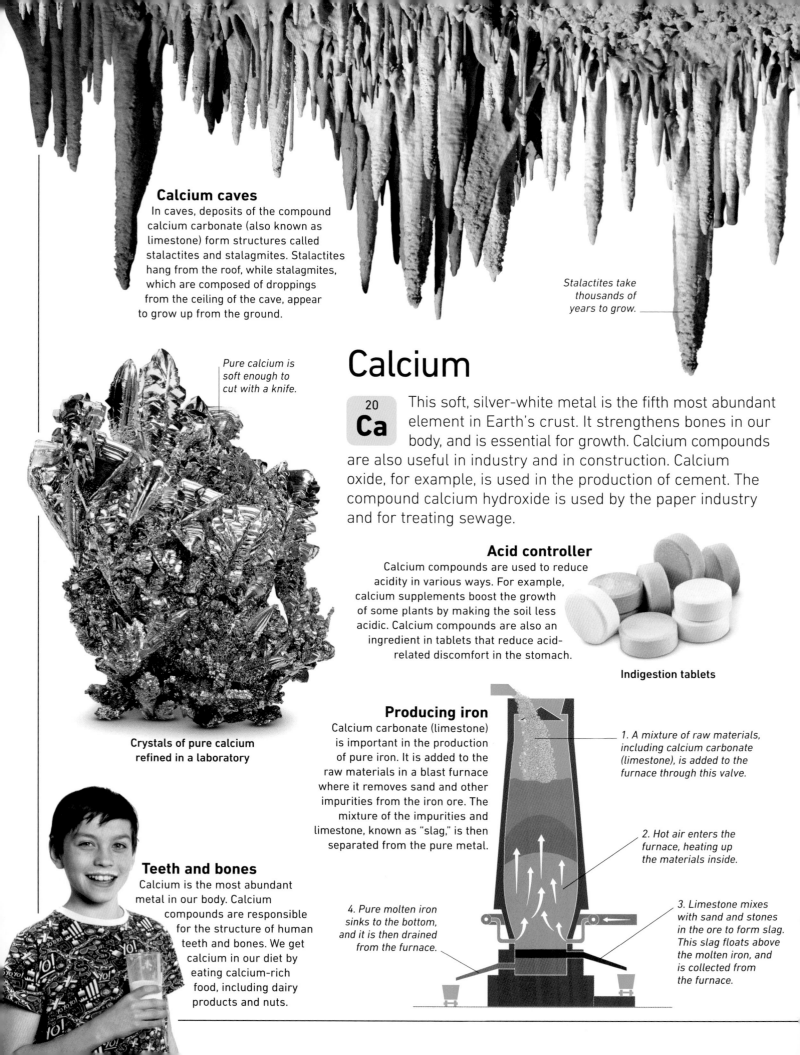

Strontium

38
Sr
This element is named after Strontian, a Scottish village near where its ore, strontianite, was discovered. Strontium has a toxic, radioactive isotope called strontium-90. Nuclear accidents, such as the 1986 disaster in Chernobyl, Ukraine, have released a large amount of strontium-90 into the atmosphere.

Signal flare
Compounds of many group 2 elements are known for their ability to produce colored flames. Calcium compounds give an orange-red color, while barium compounds are green. Strontium compounds provide a bright crimson color to fireworks and also signal flares used to attract attention (as pictured).

Barium

56
Ba
Discovered in 1808 by the English scientist Humphry Davy, the name of this highly reactive metal comes from the Greek word *barys*, meaning "heavy." Interestingly, it is not barium itself that is heavy, but the minerals (such as barite) in which it is found.

Barium meal
In this medical test, a patient is asked to swallow a "meal" of barium sulfate, a harmless compound that passes through the digestive tract. This allows a patient's digestive organs—highlighted by the barium compound—to be examined clearly using an X-ray photograph.

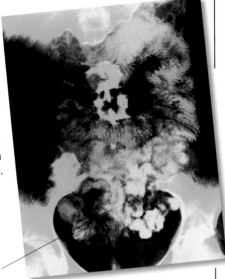

X-ray of a healthy human digestive tract, highlighted using a "barium meal."

Radium

88
Ra
A very radioactive element, radium gets its name from the Latin word *radius*, meaning "ray" (radium glows in the dark). In the early 20th century, radium compounds were used in medicines because people believed that radium cured diseases. However, its use was phased out when people who took these medicines became ill.

Glow in the dark
An isotope of radium, radium-226, was an ingredient in luminous paints used to make watch and clock dials glow in the dark. The paints became popular in the 1920s, long before the health risk was fully understood. Many people, especially young women, who worked with this paint became sick and even died as a result of exposure to radium.

The radium in this paint makes the numbers glow green-blue in the dark.

This ore contains 0.02 oz (0.7 g) of radium in every 2,205 lb (1,000 kg) of rock.

Uraninite
Formerly known as pitchblende, this mineral was the source that Marie Curie used to discover radium. By processing huge amounts of uraninite and analyzing it, she discovered both radium and polonium in uraninite samples. The radium present in the mineral is formed as a result of the radioactive decay of uranium.

Marie Curie
In 1898, Polish-born French scientist Marie Curie discovered radium and polonium, sharing credit for the former discovery with her husband, Pierre Curie. She received the Nobel Prize in Chemistry in 1911 for the discovery of these two elements.

Medal made in 1967 to commemorate the 100th anniversary of Marie Curie's birth.

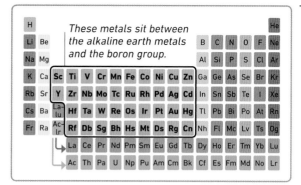

These metals sit between the alkaline earth metals and the boron group.

Transition Metals

With 38 members, the transition metals form the largest set of elements in the periodic table. They include those that sit from periods (rows) 3 to 6 and groups (columns) 3 to 12. While characteristics may vary among the members of this collection, there are some similarities. For example, these metals are typically hard and shiny, have high melting and boiling points, and are good conductors of heat and electricity.

Titanium

22 Ti Named after the titans of Greek mythology—gods who were known for their exceptional strength—titanium is a hard and strong but lightweight metal. It's a fitting name, since most of the metal's applications are based on titanium having the highest strength-to-weight ratio of all metals, and its ability to resist corrosion.

Laboratory sample of pure titanium

Shine fades to gray when element is exposed to air.

Everyday use
Titanium is used to make items where strength is important but the weight of the object must be kept low. This metal has replaced steel and aluminum in many everyday items, such as racing bicycles and glasses frames. Titanium's durability also makes it popular in alloys, to create stronger steel.

Lightweight titanium frame is durable and resistant to impact.

Glasses with titanium frames

Artificial arm made of titanium and carbon fiber

Artificial parts
This strong element is used in the medical industry to repair and even replace bones, joints, and limbs that have been damaged or lost. Titanium plates, screws, and rods can also hold bones together as they heal. The metal's resistance to corrosion is also an important characteristic in medical applications.

Scandium

Sc 21

This transition metal is very expensive and therefore has limited applications beyond research. It is used in metal alloys, where small amounts of scandium can significantly change the property of another metal, making it more useful.

Lightweight strength

Scandium can dramatically strengthen the metal aluminum, even when added in tiny amounts. One such application of the scandium–aluminum alloy is in the building of fighter jets, for which high strength and low weight are crucial.

Scandium is shiny, but quickly tarnishes in air.

Parts of this MiG-29 jet's fuselage are composed of a scandium–aluminum alloy.

Laboratory sample of pure scandium

Vanadium

V 23

A typical example of a transition metal, vanadium exhibits many of the common properties of the metals in this group. For example, it is used as a catalyst in industrial applications, as an alloy to dramatically strengthen other metals, and to form colored compounds.

These brittle crystals are the main source of vanadium.

Vanadinite

Vanadium is extracted from an ore called vanadinite. The shiny red crystals are a naturally occurring compound made of vanadium, lead, oxygen, and chlorine.

Vanadinite

Chromium

Cr 24

Like vanadium, chromium can also form many colorful compounds—chromium is what gives the gemstone ruby its bright red color. The element was once an ingredient in pigments such as chrome yellow, but it is no longer used because it is toxic.

Chrome finish

When plated on top of another metal, chromium gives machinery a polished, mirror look called the "chrome" finish. This was popular in the car industry in the 1950s and 1960s.

Chrome-plated body does not corrode easily.

1967 Shelby Cobra AC Roadster 427 sports car

Manganese

Mn 25

The Swedish chemist Johan Gottlieb Gahn discovered manganese in 1774. This element is essential in our diet in small quantities. Cereals, nuts, beets, and various other fruits and vegetables, such as blueberries, avocados, and olives, are all good sources of this transition metal.

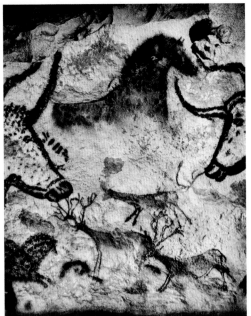

Cave art
Many pigments used in ancient paintings, such as the Lascaux cave paintings in France, come from compounds containing manganese. Oxides of manganese tend to produce brown and black colors.

Laboratory sample of pure manganese

This silvery metal is dense and brittle.

Better gasoline
A complex compound of manganese, carbon, hydrogen, and oxygen—known as MMT— is added to gasoline in order to enhance its performance. The compound boosts the octane number of the gasoline. Octane numbers are used as a measure of the efficiency of gasoline: the higher the octane number, the better the fuel.

High-quality gasoline protects motor engines from wear.

Iron

Fe 26

Based on the huge quantity produced, iron is by far the most important metal used in the world today. While construction is its most common application, iron is also used as a catalyst in many industrial processes, such as in the manufacture of ammonia for fertilizers. In human blood, iron is present in hemoglobin, a compound that carries oxygen around the body.

Iron power
When forged into weapons and machinery, iron brought economic and political power to many past empires. In the modern world, it is the main construction material, often in the form of steel—an alloy of iron and carbon— but also as cast and wrought iron.

The Eiffel Tower, Paris, France

Wrought iron lattice

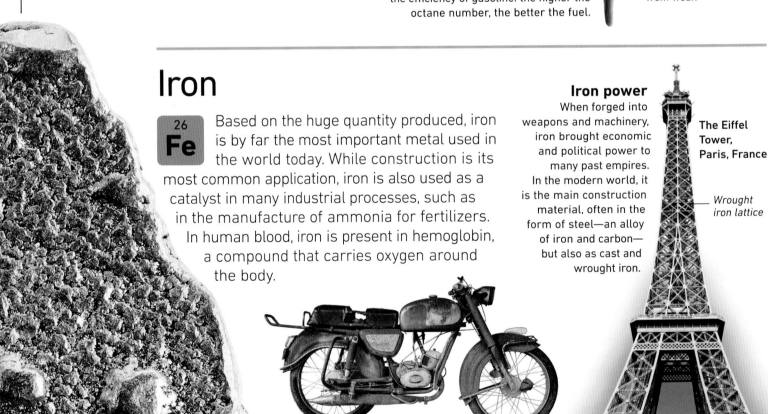

Chunk of pure iron refined in a laboratory

Rust red
Iron corrodes in a natural chemical process called oxidation, commonly known as rusting. When exposed to water or oxygen in the air, the metal's surface gets coated with a reddish-orange layer of oxide that cracks and flakes away. Left unchecked, the process can wear away all the iron.

Purple-pink crystals

Cobalt

27 Co

Like iron, cobalt is used to make permanent magnets (magnets that cannot lose their magnetism). Cobalt is important biologically—it is a part of vitamin B12, which helps prevent certain blood disorders. Alloys containing cobalt are hard-wearing and are used commercially to make jet engine blades and prosthetic body parts.

Coloring glass
In ancient times, a popular use of cobalt was in a pigment for coloring porcelain. In modern times, cobalt is often used to give glass a bright blue color.

This stained glass gets its blue color from cobalt.

Erythrite
A compound of cobalt, arsenic, oxygen, and water, erythrite is a mineral ore of cobalt. Bright red and purple, it is striking in appearance and known by miners as "cobalt bloom."

Irradiating food
One particular form (isotope) of cobalt, cobalt-60, emits gamma radiation that can be used to sterilize surgical instruments and to preserve food. When food is exposed to this type of radiation, harmful germs are killed, making the food stay fresh for a long time.

Table lamp with blue glass lampshade

Nickel

28 Ni

This element's name comes from the old German word *kupfernickel*, meaning "copper demon." At first, German miners thought this mineral contained copper. It was later found to be an ore of nickel, but the shortened name—nickel—stuck. Pure nickel does not rust and is used to coat metal objects to protect them from corrosion.

Pure nickel balls refined in a laboratory

These silvery-white pellets have a yellowish tinge.

Tagging sea turtles
Nickel alloys are used to make numbered tags that help scientists to track and identify individual marine creatures, such as sea turtles. Monel tags, as they are known, are mixtures of nickel and copper, and are highly resistant to corrosion in water.

Copper nickel
The US 5-cent coin called the "nickel" is in fact made mostly of copper. However, nickel does appear in most "silver" coinage in the form of cupronickel, the alloy that nickel forms with copper.

The George Washington quarter, also made of cupronickel, was created in 1932 to commemorate the 200th anniversary of the president's birth.

Copper

Cu 29

Found in minerals such as malachite, the color of pure copper makes it easily recognizable among metals. This element is very malleable and a good conductor of electricity. For this reason, it is useful in roofing, water pipes, coins, and electric motors.

Pellets of pure copper refined in a laboratory

Green lady

Verdigris, a mixture of several copper compounds, is the green coating that forms on copper when it is exposed to air. The Statue of Liberty, in New York City, is now green because of verdigris on its copper layer.

Verdigris-coated copper layer sits on an iron framework.

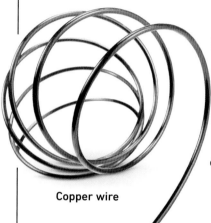

Electrical wires

Copper is a natural choice for use in circuits and electrical wiring because of its ductility (the ability to be drawn out into thin wires) and its excellent electrical conductivity.

Copper wire

Making music

When mixed with zinc, copper forms an alloy called brass, which has long been used for making musical instruments. Because copper can be shaped easily, brass can be formed into complicated shapes to make these instruments—they also have a good acoustic quality and are very durable.

Brass saxophone

Zinc

Zn 30

A relatively common metal, zinc can be obtained from minerals such as sphalerite and smithsonite. This element is useful in many ways, mainly in compound form. Apart from being present in the alloy brass, its major use is in preventing the corrosion of steel. Its compound zinc oxide is commonly used as a white sunscreen cream.

Laboratory sample of pure zinc

In our diet

Zinc is essential in our diet. We consume it in foods such as cheese and sunflower seeds. Red meat—in the form of beef, liver, and lamb—is a particularly good source of zinc, as are herrings and oysters.

Sunflower seeds

This garden bucket's steel surface is galvanized to keep it safe from corrosion.

Protecting steel

Steel can be shielded from corrosion by coating it with zinc—a process known as galvanization. The outer layer of zinc forms a barrier around the steel underneath, protecting it from constant exposure to water.

Galvanized bucket

Yttrium

39 Y Along with three other elements— ytterbium, erbium, and terbium—yttrium is named after the town of Ytterby, in Sweden. Yttrium has a radioactive form, yttrium-90, which is used widely in treating several types of cancers.

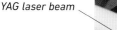

Laboratory sample of pure yttrium

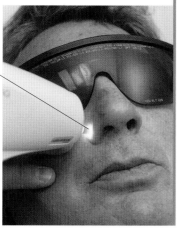

YAG laser beam

Medical laser

When combined with other elements, yttrium can be used in laser surgery. A YAG (yttrium aluminum garnet) laser, when combined with an element called neodymium, is useful for cosmetic treatments such as skin laser therapy.

Zirconium

Bar of pure zirconium refined in a laboratory

40 Zr This element gets its name from the Arabic word *zargun*, meaning "gold." This is because its main mineral source, zircon, has a brownish-golden color. A shiny metal, zirconium is used to make hard-wearing alloys, such as those fitted in the outer layer of fuel rods in nuclear reactors.

Fake diamonds

Cubic zirconia, the crystalline form of zirconium dioxide, can mimic diamonds. These fake diamonds can also appear in various colors using other elements—for example, erbium makes pink cubic zirconia.

Molybdenum

42 Mo Discovered in 1781 by the Swedish chemist Peter Jacob Hjelm, molybdenum is an essential element in our diet. It is found in foods such as lentils and beans, and it helps clear some toxins from the body. One of its most important industrial uses is in the production of moly-steels— steel alloys that have molybdenum added to them to make them harder and more resilient.

Element of war

Both the British and German armies used molybdenum during World War I. While the British used it to protect their tanks, the Germans used it for their heavy artillery.

British World War I Mark IV tank

Chunk of pure molybdenum refined in a laboratory

Steel-molybdenum body forms a protective layer against enemy fire.

Niobium

Nb 41

Sourced mainly from the mineral columbite, this transition metal was known as "columbium" for more than 150 years in the US. It has many uses: from pacemaker cases for the human heart to commemorative coins, jet engines, and rocket parts. Niobium-based magnets are used in MRI machines for medical imaging.

Rods of pure niobium refined in a laboratory

Artist's representation of the Apollo 15 Command/ Service Module (CSM) spacecraft

This expansion nozzle was made of a niobium alloy.

Space exploration

Niobium is often mixed with other metals for specialized applications. Niobium was used in making parts of the Apollo 15 Command/ Service Module spacecraft. The Apollo 15 mission was the fourth one to land humans on the Moon.

Technetium

Tc 43

Originally thought not to occur in nature, it was later discovered that tiny amounts of technetium do exist as the result of the natural radioactive decay of uranium. In such small quantities, it was not easy to find the element. Mendeleev predicted its existence as a missing element on his original periodic table. There followed many false claims of discovery, before technetium was finally confirmed in 1937. Today, it is used mainly in medical imaging.

Ruthenium

Ru 44

This transition metal is extracted from the minerals pentlandite and pyroxenite. Ruthenium is often combined with platinum to harden electrical components. The element can also help speed up the industrial production of ammonia, a key ingredient in fertilizers.

Bright, silvery metal

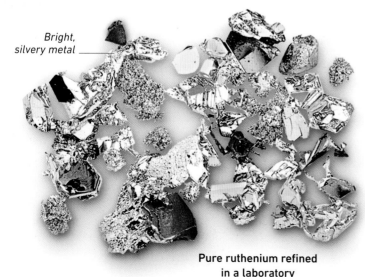

Pure ruthenium refined in a laboratory

Rhodium

Rh 45

In industry, this rare and hard metal is mainly obtained as a byproduct during the refining of nickel and copper. One of rhodium's main applications is in making catalytic converters—devices that convert harmful exhaust gases into less dangerous ones—for cars. It is also used in many alloys to increase their resistance to corrosion.

Rhodium-coated mirror makes the reflection of an object precise and sharp.

Pure rhodium pellet refined in a laboratory

Special mirrors

Rhodium's ability to be polished to a bright shine allows it to be used in industrial and specialized mirrors. For example, the mouth mirrors used by dentists often contain rhodium.

Pure palladium bar
refined in a laboratory

Steel-gray mineral

Palladium

46
Pd

Among the precious metals, palladium is far rarer than silver or gold. It is used extensively in jewelry, particularly in "white gold" where gold is mixed with other silver-colored metals. A curious property of palladium is its ability to soak up hydrogen gas: at room temperature, it can absorb up to 900 times its own volume of hydrogen. In the future, therefore, this metal could be used to store hydrogen for fuel.

Catalytic converter
Palladium is often used to coat the insides of catalytic converters for cars. Harmful gases such as carbon monoxide, some hydrocarbons, and various oxides go through the catalytic converter, react with the palladium coating, and are converted to carbon dioxide, water, and nitrogen. These are then released into the air through the car's exhaust systems.

Braggite
Although palladium is found pure in nature, it also appears in some rare minerals, such as braggite. Discovered in 1932, this mineral also contains platinum, nickel, and sulfur.

Silver

Pellet of pure silver

Crystal-like structure

47
Ag

This precious metal has been used for centuries, both as a form of currency and to craft jewelry. As the compound silver nitrate, it has been used as an antibiotic and a disinfectant. Some silver compounds, such as silver bromide, are light-sensitive; they change color when exposed to light. This property made the development of black-and-white photography possible.

Chlorargyrite
One of the main ores of silver, chlorargyrite is chiefly composed of the compound silver chloride. It is colorless until it is exposed to light, when it turns brown and purple.

Using silver
Due to its shiny appearance, silver has been used in jewelry and in decorative items, from candlesticks to utensils. One drawback of silver is that when exposed to air, it tarnishes easily to produce black-colored silver sulfide. As a result, decorative items that contain silver need to be cleaned regularly.

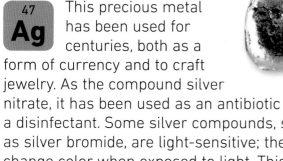

Cadmium

48 Cd This element was discovered in 1817 in a mineral called calamine. In its pure form, the soft metal is silvery with a bluish tinge. Once a common ingredient in a variety of products, such as paint, cadmium is now known to be toxic and is used less and less.

This brittle mineral is easily chipped.

Smithsonite
Named after the English chemist James Smithson, this mineral was first identified in 1802. Smithsonite mainly contains white zinc carbonate, but cadmium impurities give it a bright yellow color.

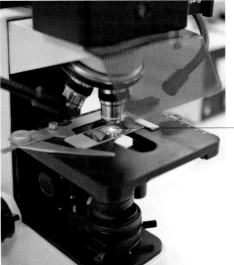

Ultraviolet (UV) light in this microscope is produced by a cadmium laser.

Pure cadmium pellet refined in a laboratory

High-intensity lasers
Powerful optical microscopes use cadmium lasers to study tiny specimens, such as microscopic organisms. The data collected by these lasers can then be pieced together to create 3-D images of the specimens, so scientists can study them further.

Hafnium

72 Hf Dmitri Mendeleev's prediction in 1869 of the existence of "element 72" encouraged Dutch physicist Dirk Coster and Hungarian radiologist Georg Karl von Hevesy to study zirconium ores. They discovered hafnium in 1923, and named it after *Hafnia*—the Latin name for Denmark's capital Copenhagen—the city where it was discovered.

Pure hafnium is resistant to corrosion in air.

Rods of pure tantalum refined in a laboratory

Tantalum shell is flexible and lightweight.

Walking easy
Tantalum body implants are more porous than titanium, which helps them flex like natural bones. This encourages bone growth, which keeps the implants firmly in place. Its ability to mimic the elasticity of bones has made tantalum an excellent choice for patients who need an artificial joint.

Artificial hip implant

Tantalum

73 Ta A hard metal that does not corrode easily, tantalum is combined with softer metals to make them stronger. Capacitors—devices used to store electric charge—in gadgets such as cell phones are often made of tantalum powder. The metal is also widely used to make high-quality artificial joints.

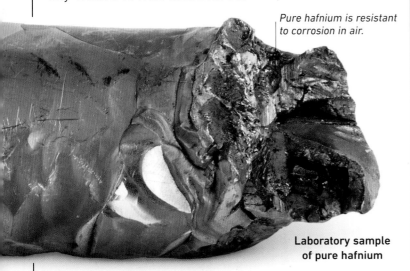

Laboratory sample of pure hafnium

This mineral is the main ore of tungsten.

Drill bit strengthened with the alloy tungsten carbide

Wolframite

Osmium

76 Os

The pure form of osmium turns into a poisonous oxide when it reacts with oxygen in the air. For safe use, it is combined with other elements. From fingerprint powder used in forensic laboratories to nibs for fountain pens, osmium alloys have many specialized uses.

Fountain pen

The nib of this fountain pen is made of an osmium alloy, making it hard-wearing.

This sand is a natural alloy of osmium and iridium.

Osmiridium sand

Tungsten

74 W

Heavy and dense, tungsten has the highest melting point of any metal. Compared to gold, which melts at 1,947.2°F (1,064°C), tungsten turns to liquid at 6,177.2°F (3,414°C). Its resistance to heat is useful in making light bulb filaments, although they are not very energy-efficient.

Rhenium

75 Re

Named after the Rhine River in Germany, this element was discovered in 1925. It has the second highest melting point of all metals. Rhenium's ability to withstand high heat has made it very effective in superalloys used in oven filaments, X-ray machines, and jet aircraft turbine blades.

Pure rhenium pellet refined in a laboratory

Iridium

77 Ir

In nature, iridium is found in sediments deposited by rivers. A thin layer of iridium is also present in Earth's crust. Some scientists believe that the same meteorite that triggered the death of the dinosaurs 66 million years ago distributed this layer of iridium across Earth with its impact.

Powerful telescope

NASA's Chandra X-ray Observatory, an Earth-orbiting telescope that studies X-rays from distant stars, has eight iridium-coated glass mirrors. The coating helps catch and bounce the X-rays toward the telescope's scientific instruments that study the rays and gather data.

Turbo engine

The Rolls-Royce Trent XWB is a turbofan jet engine used on the Airbus A350 XWB aeroplane. Its inner blades, which are made of a superalloy that includes rhenium, can withstand extremely high temperatures.

Artist's impression of Chandra X-ray observatory

This silver-colored metal can be polished to a bright white finish.

Nugget of pure platinum refined in a laboratory

Platinum

78 Pt

A natural choice for making jewelry, this precious metal is quite rare in Earth's crust, which makes it expensive. It also plays an important role in industry as a catalyst; for example, in the production of nitric acid, which is used in making fertilizers.

Jewelry
As a beautiful, durable, and lustrous white metal, platinum has been sought after for making jewelry for centuries. The metal stays shiny for a long time because it has has a high resistance to corrosion.

Platinum ring

Rutherfordium

104 Rf

An artificial element, rutherfordium is made by bombarding californium atoms with carbon atoms. It was first created in the late 1960s, but it took until 1992 for it to be confirmed and named. Only a few atoms have ever been produced, and this element has no known applications outside of research.

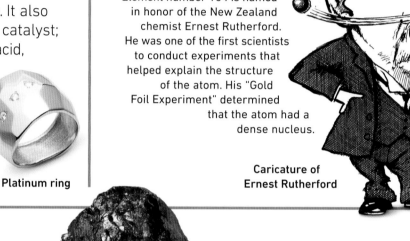

Naming rutherfordium
Element number 104 is named in honor of the New Zealand chemist Ernest Rutherford. He was one of the first scientists to conduct experiments that helped explain the structure of the atom. His "Gold Foil Experiment" determined that the atom had a dense nucleus.

Caricature of Ernest Rutherford

Mercury

80 Hg

This fascinating element was in use nearly 30,000 years ago, when ancient humans melted its mineral ore cinnabar into a red pigment to make cave paintings. It is the only metal that is liquid at room temperature, and was often known as "quicksilver" because of the way it flows.

Striking, deep-red mineral

Cinnabar

Cinnabar
As the main ore of mercury, cinnabar has been used for thousands of years. In 16th-century China, for example, craftsmen painted small wooden jewelry boxes with the bright red pigment extracted from cinnabar. This mineral was also once crushed into a powdered form for use as a cosmetic. Over the centuries, its use has declined due to mercury's toxicity.

Dense, silver-white liquid at room temperature

Mercury thermometer
Polish-born Dutch physicist Daniel Gabriel Fahrenheit invented the mercury thermometer in 1714. His name is given to the Fahrenheit temperature scale that is used in the US. In a mercury thermometer, the mercury expands and rises up the narrow tube as the temperature increases. Because of concerns over the toxicity of mercury, these thermometers are being gradually replaced by safe, digital versions.

Gold

79 Au

The chemical symbol for this element comes from the Latin word *aurum*, meaning "gold." This metal is found in its pure form, and has been used in jewelry and decoration for nearly 4,000 years. Alchemists—the forerunners of modern chemists—sought to convert relatively common metals such as lead into precious ones like gold.

Gold vein

Gold in quartz

In some rivers, gold erodes and breaks up into flakes. Eventually, these tiny flakes transfer to a hard mineral called quartz, and build up to produce large veins of the shiny gold metal.

Gold used as a reflective screen

Reflecting heat

The Sun's heat can be dangerous to equipment or astronauts in space. As a safety measure, an astronaut wears a helmet with a visor covered with a thin layer of gold. This protective coating reflects the Sun's intense, harmful rays away from the astronaut's face and prevents overheating.

Flakes of pure gold refined in a laboratory

Coins of gold

Pure gold, and alloys that include gold, have been used in coins since ancient times. Its shiny appearance, high value-to-weight ratio, and ability to resist corrosion made it a popular choice for use as money.

Coin issued by King Philip II of Macedonia (359–336 BCE)

The gold covering the Golden Temple in Amritsar, India, is not only decorative, it also resists corrosion.

Decorating with gold

Gold does not tarnish over time and as such has been used in buildings by architects since ancient times as an adornment. Gold leaf work and gold plating are common forms of decorations. The metal can even be used in flake and dust form to decorate food for consumption in some parts of the world, such as India.

Dubnium

105 Db Named after Dubna, the Russian town where it was first made, element number 105 is radioactive. Dubnium is an artificial element and currently has no uses beyond scientific research.

Albert Ghiorso (right) with James Harris, a fellow scientist

Controversial discovery

Two teams of scientists, one from Russia and the other from the US, claimed to have made dubnium at different times. The team in Russia was led by Georgy Flerov in 1968, and the American team was led by Albert Ghiorso in 1970. It wasn't until 1993 that the Russian team was credited with the discovery, and dubnium was officially named.

Seaborgium

106 Sg Only a few atoms of this artificial element have ever been made. They were first created in 1974 at the Lawrence Berkeley National Laboratory, California, by making californium atoms collide with oxygen atoms. Seaborgium is currently used only in scientific research.

Naming seaborgium

American chemist Glenn T. Seaborg worked with various teams during his career, creating many artificial elements. At the time, it was unusual to name an element after a living person, but he was honored in this way in 1993, before his death in 1999.

Cartoon of Seaborg at a blackboard

Bohrium

107 Bh Like many other artificial elements, bohrium is used only in scientific research. It was discovered in 1981 by a team of German scientists firing chromium atoms at those of bismuth to make one atom of bohrium. This element was named after the Danish physicist Niels Bohr in 1997.

Niels Bohr in his laboratory

Niels Bohr

The Danish physicist Niels Bohr is best known for his pioneering work on the structure of the atom and his insight into atomic theory. His famous "Bohr model" of the atom earned him the Nobel Prize in Physics in 1922.

Hassium

108 Hs This element was named after the German state of Hesse, which is home to the Center for Heavy Ion Research—the institution where hassium was made in 1984. To create hassium, a team of scientists, led by the German physicist Peter Armbruster, crashed lead and iron atoms together. Like all of the super-heavy artificial elements, hassium's atoms are radioactive, meaning that they quickly decay to form other elements.

Meitnerium

Named in honor of the Austrian physicist Lise Meitner, meitnerium was first created in Germany in 1982, when atoms of bismuth and iron were smashed into one another. This radioactive element has no known uses outside research.

Meitner and Hahn
The German chemist Otto Hahn alone won the Nobel Prize for Chemistry in 1944 for the work he and Meitner did together on nuclear fission. Meitner, meanwhile, went on to have the honor of this new element being named for her, 24 years after her death.

Otto Hahn (left) and Lise Meitner

Darmstadtium

First created in 1994 in the German city of Darmstadt, darmstadtium was later named after this city. Only a few atoms of this highly radioactive element have ever been made. because they break apart quickly, little is known about this element.

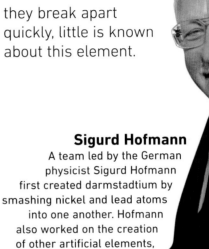

Sigurd Hofmann
A team led by the German physicist Sigurd Hofmann first created darmstadtium by smashing nickel and lead atoms into one another. Hofmann also worked on the creation of other artificial elements, such as roentgenium and copernicium.

Roentgenium

Because this element is placed directly below gold on the periodic table, some scientists believe it is likely to share some of gold's characteristics. It was first made in 1994 by smashing together nickel and bismuth atoms. Roentgenium has no current applications other than in scientific research.

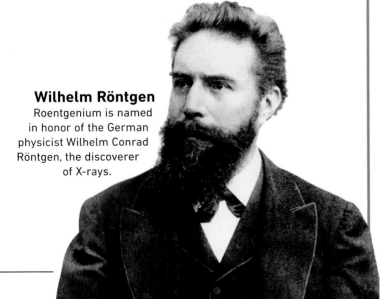

Wilhelm Röntgen
Roentgenium is named in honor of the German physicist Wilhelm Conrad Röntgen, the discoverer of X-rays.

Copernicium

A highly radioactive element, copernicium was first made in 1996 when atoms of zinc were made to collide with lead atoms. Some scientists think it is unreactive, like a noble gas, but only a few of its atoms have ever been produced, so there is no research to back up that theory.

Paying homage
Copernicium was named after the 16th-century Polish astronomer Nicolaus Copernicus, who came up with the theory that Earth moves around the Sun. This is a statue of him in front of Olsztyn Castle, where he lived.

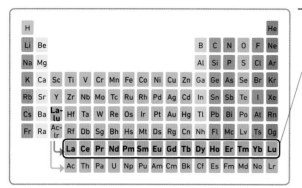

The lanthanide series—the collective name for elements 57–70—is named after lanthanum, the first element in this series.

Lanthanum

57 La

This lanthanide was discovered by the Swedish chemist Carl Gustav Mosander in 1839. One of its compounds—lanthanum oxide—is added to the glass in some camera lenses to improve image quality. Scientists can determine the age of ancient rocks by comparing the relative amounts of lanthanum and one of its decay products, barium, in the rocks.

Lanthanides

Once known as the "rare earths," the lanthanides are in fact not rare at all. The chemistry of many of the lanthanide elements is similar in many cases, and, as a result, they have proven difficult to separate from one another. Indeed, in Greek, *lanthano* means "hidden." They have a wide range of applications.

Bastnasite
This mineral is a mixture of three metals: yttrium, cerium, and lanthanum, combined with carbon, oxygen, and fluorine. Bastnasite is used as a source of each of those elements, which are extracted from the ore in a complex process.

Neodymium

60 Nd

In 1885, the Austrian chemist Carl Auer von Welsbach extracted this element from didymium, a mixture of neodymium and praseodymium. It is one of the components used to create lasers that aid in eye surgery.

This silvery-white metal will tarnish quickly in air.

Laboratory sample of pure neodymium

Promethium

61 Pm

Because of its radioactivity, promethium is not typically found in naturally occurring minerals. Any promethium in nature would have decayed over time but this lanthanide can be made artificially. Small amounts of it are used in special batteries, which have a wide range of uses, from heart pacemakers to military missiles.

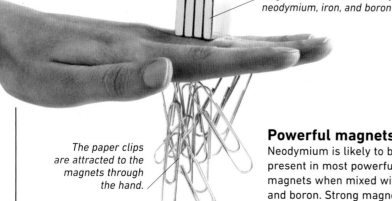

Magnets made from an alloy of neodymium, iron, and boron

The paper clips are attracted to the magnets through the hand.

Powerful magnets
Neodymium is likely to be present in most powerful magnets when mixed with iron and boron. Strong magnets have many industrial applications.

Promethium-rich paint

Paints
Mixed with zinc sulfide, promethium is added to paint to give a green-blue glow. The manufacture of "glow in the dark" watch dials using promethium was once popular, but this application has been largely phased out.

Cerium

58 Ce In 1803, cerium was discovered and named after Ceres, which is now known to be a dwarf planet. Cerium is found in a number of naturally occurring minerals, such as cerite, a mineral composed mainly of cerium silicate. A compound called cerium oxide is used in catalytic converters (devices that convert harmful exhaust gases into less harmful ones) in cars.

Laboratory sample of pure cerium

Praseodymium

59 Pr A part of praseodymium's name comes from the Greek word *prasios*, meaning "green." It was named so because of the green color of the oxide it forms on reaction with air. When mixed with magnesium, praseodymium makes a strong alloy that is used in aircraft engines.

Laboratory sample of pure praseodymium

These glasses from the 1920s contain praseodymium that makes them green.

A filter for protective glasses
Praseodymium is used to give a colored tint to the safety glasses used by welders and glassblowers. The tinted goggles filter out the potentially damaging ultraviolet radiation, protecting the wearer's eyes.

Samarium

62 Sm This element was named after the mineral samarskite, from which it was first extracted. Some early, specialized magnets were made of samarium mixed with cobalt. These magnets were useful because they continued to be magnetic even at high temperatures.

Laboratory samples of pure samarium

Europium

63 Eu Discovered in 1901 by the French chemist Eugène-Anatole Demarçay, europium's best known application is in the inks that are used to print bank notes. Printed with this ink, a genuine Euro note glows red under ultraviolet light. This helps banks detect forged currency.

Laboratory sample of pure europium

Gadolinium

64 Gd Named after the Finnish chemist Johan Gadolin, gadolinium can be mixed with some other elements to make magnets. It can also help iron alloys resist high temperatures.

Laboratory sample of pure gadolinium

Soft, silvery metal

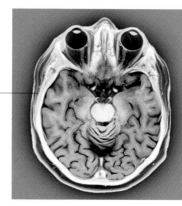

Gadolinium MRI scan of a healthy human brain and eyes

Gadolinite
This ore contains tiny amounts of gadolinium, and forms black or dark brown crystals. Other elements in it include lanthanum, cerium, neodymium, and yttrium.

Clear images
Gadolinium is used in MRI (magnetic resonance imaging) scans as a contrasting agent to help improve the quality of the images of internal body structures. However, the element is toxic, so must be used with care.

Terbium

65 Tb Discovered in 1843 by the Swedish chemist Carl Mosander, terbium is one of four elements named after the tiny Swedish village of Ytterby—the other elements are erbium, yttrium, and ytterbium. Because of the similarity in their names and properties, scientists confused the elements terbium and erbium in the 19th century, calling each by the name of the other. Apart from being used in mercury lamps and low-energy light bulbs, terbium can also produce green phosphors—compounds that are still used to light up color televisions.

Dysprosium

66 Dy The Greek word *dysprosistos*, for which dysprosium is named, means "hard to get at." Like other lanthanides, this element occurs in nature combined with other members of its group, and is difficult to extract. Despite its discovery in 1886, dysprosium was not isolated until the 1950s. Rarely used in its pure form, it is mainly used in alloys.

Generating energy
Dysprosium's main commercial use today is as an alloy with neodymium, praseodymium, and terbium in making powerful magnets. Strong and lightweight, these magnets help run many wind turbines.

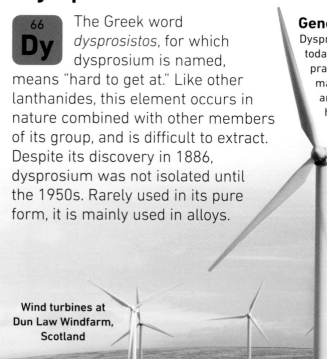

Wind turbines at Dun Law Windfarm, Scotland

Holmium

67 Ho This element is a malleable, silvery white metal. Apart from being used in alloys for making magnets, holmium is also used in some medical lasers, especially ones that break up kidney stones.

The red color in this zirconia gemstone comes from holmium oxide.

Rich color
Holmium impurities can give a red or yellow color to a zirconia gemstone. The compound holmium oxide can also be used to color glass.

Erbium

68
Er

This silvery metal is used in the form of its compound erbium oxide to add a pink color to glassware, ceramic glazes, and imitation gemstones. It is also alloyed with metals, such as vanadium, to make them softer and easier to shape.

Laboratory sample of pure erbium

These safety goggles contain erbium.

Protective goggles

Erbium oxide is added to glass used in protective goggles worn by welders and glassblowers. This glass absorbs the ultraviolet radiation that can damage our eyes.

Thulium

69
Tm

Pure thulium has a bright, silvery luster, which tarnishes on exposure to air. This element can be used to produce X-rays for portable machines commonly found in dentists' offices.

This metal is soft enough to cut with a knife.

Laboratory sample of pure thulium

Ytterbium

70
Yb

This soft metal reacts with air to form a layer of oxide compound on its surface. A small amount of ytterbium is sometimes used to strengthen steel. Its compounds are also used in lasers.

Laboratory sample of pure ytterbium

Shiny metal

Standardizing time

Inside this highly sensitive optical clock, ytterbium atoms oscillate in response to the light of a laser beam. Counting these oscillations helps keep time accurately.

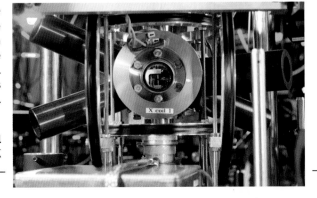

Optical clock, National Physical Laboratory, Teddington, UK

Lutetium

71
Lu

Like most other lanthanides, lutetium's principal ore is also monazite. This element is a hard, silver-colored metal with a high density. Lutetium is rare and hard to extract. As a result, it is expensive and its commercial uses are limited. Lutetium compounds are used as catalysts in chemical reactions in the petrochemical industry. One of lutetium's radioactive isotopes—lutetium 177—is used in cancer therapy.

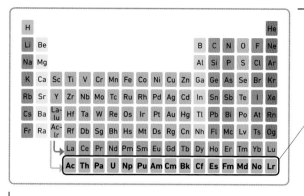

The elements with atomic numbers 89 to 103 are the actinides.

Thorium

90 Th

A relatively common element, thorium appears in many naturally occurring minerals. Special glass with thorium dioxide was once used to make high-efficiency camera lenses, but the thorium made them radioactive. Research into using thorium as a nuclear fuel is ongoing.

Brownish red mineral

Monazite
The chief ore of thorium, monazite also contains varying amounts of the elements cerium, lanthanum, gadolinium, and neodymium. Depending on the exact composition, monazite varies in color from yellow to brownish red.

Actinides

The elements in this series are fiercely radioactive metals. Most of them are either present only as decayed radioactive products, or have to be artificially created. All the elements after uranium are called "transuranium" elements, and most of them are used mainly in research.

Yellow-green crystals under visible light

Actinium

89 Ac

A radioactive element present in Earth's crust in tiny amounts, actinium is produced in the laboratory by firing neutrons at radium atoms. One of actinium's isotopes— actinium-225—is used in cancer treatment, emitting particles that attack cancer cells.

These vials for intravenous injections contain actinium, selenium, and radium.

Autunite
Actinium can be found in autunite, a mineral that contains uranium. The uranium in the rock undergoes natural radioactive decay, and in the process, it produces actinium atoms in small quantities. Autunite's crystals glow bright green under ultraviolet light.

Radioactive cures
During the early 20th century, radiation was considered by some as a cure-all for many diseases and health problems. Intravenous injections for various illnesses contained radioactive elements, including actinium. As radioactive elements and radioactivity became better understood, it was finally realized that there were terrible health consequences associated with such treatments.

Protactinium

91 Pa

The name protactinium comes from the Greek word *protos*—meaning "first"—coupled with actinium. It refers to the fact that protactinium is formed before actinium, in a radioactive decay sequence that starts with uranium. A form of protactinium is used by scientists to calculate the age of ocean sands.

Brittle, shiny ore

Torbernite

This mineral contains copper and uranium. The uranium present decays, eventually releasing protactinium in small quantities. The vivid green crystals are popular with mineral collectors, but they can release radioactive radon gas, which is a major health hazard.

William Crookes

In 1900, the English chemist William Crookes isolated protactinium from uranium, calling it uranium-X. He is also famous for the discovery of the element thallium in 1861, and for inventing the Crookes tube, an instrument that helped in the discovery of X-rays.

Neptunium

93 Np

Many scientists believed that the periodic table ended with uranium. The discovery of neptunium in 1940 was an important one, as it was the first element after uranium to be artificially created. Its discovery opened up a new world of transuranium elements. American scientists Edwin McMillan and Glenn T. Seaborg were awarded the 1951 Nobel Prize in Chemistry for this work.

Uraninite

A naturally occurring mineral, uraninite was originally known as pitchblende. It is composed chiefly of uranium compounds, but also contains small amounts of some other elements, including neptunium.

Americium

95 Am

Another artificially produced radioactive actinide, americium was first synthesized in the US in 1944. This element is only produced in nuclear reactors. It also emits rays that can be used to monitor the thickness of metal sheets in industry.

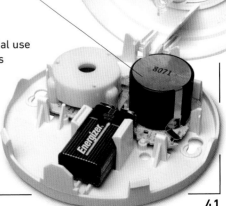

The sensor in this smoke detector contains tiny amounts of radioactive americium.

Detecting smoke

Americium's main commercial use is in smoke alarms. It creates an electrical current inside a smoke detector and if smoke interferes with the current, an alarm sounds. When the smoke clears and the current is reestablished, the alarm turns off.

41

Uranium

92 U This silvery gray element changed the course of history. Its impact on the world, both in terms of its use as a nuclear fuel and in nuclear weapons, has been enormous. The discovery of radioactivity by the Nobel Prize-winning French physicist Henri Becquerel, through his study of uranium, opened the door to the nuclear age.

Chunk of pure uranium

Mining uranium

The Ranger uranium mine in the Northern Territory of Australia (above) is one of the world's largest sources of uranium. This element is widely available in ores—including uraninite and carnotite—in Earth's crust. Once extracted from the ground, the ore undergoes a complex process of chemical reactions that turn it into uranium oxide. This compound is turned into a fuel used in nuclear reactors.

Mushroom cloud

Since World War II, scientists have been able to harness uranium to create nuclear bombs. This process, called fission, occurs when a neutron in a particular form (isotope) of uranium strikes the atom's nucleus, splitting it to release an enormous amount of energy. This chain reaction becomes self-sustaining as neutrons created by that first split atom strike more nuclei. The resulting, often deadly, atomic explosion looks like a massive mushroom cloud.

This glaze contains up to 14 percent uranium.

Radioactive red

Fiestaware was a range of ceramics that were popular in the 1930s. The red glazes that were applied to the plates, cups, and saucers, included a significant amount of uranium oxide, which made them radioactive. The glaze was eventually discontinued.

This mushroom cloud was created in 1953 after an atomic bomb explosion at a test site in Nevada.

Plutonium

94 Pu Much like uranium, plutonium is used as a nuclear fuel—its most common application. Named after the dwarf planet Pluto, very little of this element exists in nature, so it has to be made artificially. It was discovered in 1940 in Berkeley, California, but its discovery was kept a secret until 1946 because the Americans were concerned about national security, and plutonium's use in a nuclear weapon.

Glowing piece of plutonium oxide, the plutonium compound used as a nuclear fuel

Replica of the "Fat Man" bomb, US Air Force Museum and National Aviation Hall of Fame, Ohio.

Codename: Fat Man

Nuclear weapons were dropped by the US on Japan at the end of World War II. The plutonium-based "Fat Man" atomic bomb was dropped on the city of Nagasaki in August 1945, just a few days after a uranium-based bomb was dropped on Hiroshima. The devastating nuclear fission reaction that took place in Nagasaki involved plutonium atoms splitting apart to release huge amounts of energy.

Artist's representation of the *New Horizons* spacecraft passing Pluto

Far from Earth

Launched in 2006 to study the dwarf planet Pluto, the *New Horizons* spacecraft carried about 24 lb (10.9 kg) of radioactive plutonium—enough fuel to keep its instruments running for 10 years. *New Horizons* made its closest approach to Pluto in July 2015.

Curium

96 Cm This radioactive element was named in honor of the Polish-born chemist Marie Curie and her French husband, Pierre. Curium was discovered by the American chemist Glenn T. Seaborg at the University of California, Berkeley, in 1944. He produced this element in a cyclotron, a machine that smashes atoms into one another.

Marie Curie conducting an experiment in her laboratory.

Californium

98 Cf Named after the state of California, californium was discovered in 1950 by the American scientists Stanley Thompson, Kenneth Street Jr., Albert Ghiorso, and Glenn T. Seaborg. This radioactive element is used in the treatment of cancer. It is also employed in portable metal detectors.

Artificial creation
These pellets of californium were refined in a laboratory. The element is not found in nature and is created artificially by smashing atoms of berkelium with neutrons.

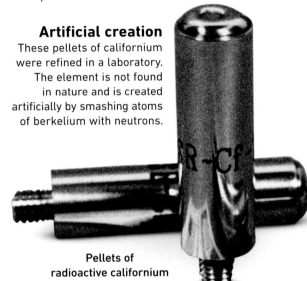

Pellets of radioactive californium

Berkelium

97 Bk This radioactive, silvery-white metal was named after the city of Berkeley in California, where it was first made. In 1949, its discovery was led by a team of three American researchers—Glenn T. Seaborg, Stanley Thompson, and Albert Ghiorso. This element is so rare that it has no commercial or technological use today. In fact, only one gram of this soft lement has been synthesized in the US since 1967.

Einsteinium

99 Es Discovered in 1952, this silvery metallic element was named after the German-born physicist Albert Einstein. It was one of the two elements (along with fermium) to be identified while studying the remains of the "Ivy Mike" test—the first hydrogen bomb explosion.

Professor Albert Einstein

Fermium

100 Fm The element fermium was named after the Italian physicist Enrico Fermi, the creator of the world's first nuclear reactor. Fermium is an artificial element useful only in scientific research.

"Ivy Mike" test
The first successful test of a hydrogen bomb in the Pacific Ocean in 1952 generated tiny amounts of fermium. This bomb was 1,000 times more powerful than regular nuclear bombs of the time.

Nobelium

102 No American scientists Albert Ghiorso and John R Walton and Norwegian Torbjørn Sikkeland are credited with the discovery of this element. They created nobelium by making atoms of curium smash into carbon atoms in a cyclotron. It was named after the Swedish chemist and engineer, Alfred Nobel. Nobelium has no uses other than scientific research.

The Nobel Prize medal has Swedish inventor Alfred Nobel's face embossed on it.

Mendelevium

101 Md In 1955, a new element was produced by smashing together atoms of einsteinium and helium in a cyclotron at Berkeley in California. This radioactive element was named after Dmitri Mendeleev, the creator of the modern periodic table. Mendelevium is used only in scientific research.

Russian chemist and inventor Dmitri Mendeleev

Lawrencium

103 Lr Like many other artificially created elements, lawrencium is used only in scientific research. The American nuclear physicist Albert Ghiorso discovered lawrencium at the Lawrence Berkeley National Laboratory, California, by firing boron atoms at californium atoms in a cyclotron. This element was named in honor of Ernest Lawrence, inventor of the cyclotron.

American physicist Ernest Lawrence with a cyclotron

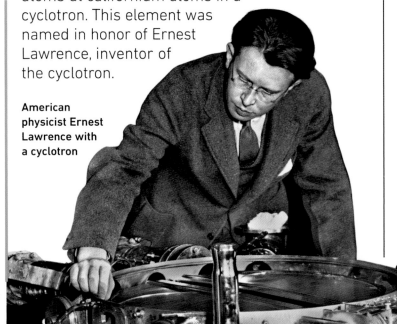

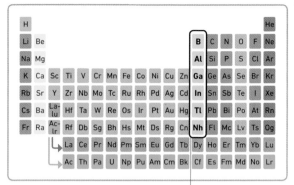

Group 13 of the periodic table houses the boron group.

The Boron Group

Except for the semimetal boron, all of the elements in this group are metals. Aluminum is abundant in Earth's crust, but hard to extract. Pure gallium is shiny and soft enough to melt at room temperature. Indium forms compounds that are essential in many modern electronics, while thallium is a deadly poison. Scientists know very little about nihonium—the only artificial element in this group.

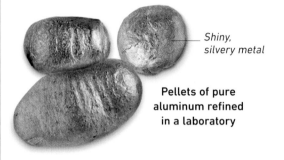

Shiny, silvery metal

Pellets of pure aluminum refined in a laboratory

Aluminum

13 Al

This element is the most abundant metal in Earth's crust, and the third most abundant among all elements, after oxygen and silicon. A light and strong metal, aluminum has a huge number of applications in industry and construction, particularly in building aircraft.

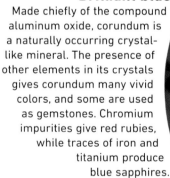

Brilliant blue

Made chiefly of the compound aluminum oxide, corundum is a naturally occurring crystal-like mineral. The presence of other elements in its crystals gives corundum many vivid colors, and some are used as gemstones. Chromium impurities give red rubies, while traces of iron and titanium produce blue sapphires.

Blue sapphire

Greenish-blue surface is soft and scratches easily.

Variscite

Many aluminum ores occur naturally. Variscite is formed when water rich in phosphates—naturally occurring compounds of phosphorus—reacts with aluminum-rich rocks. A striking green-blue colored mineral, variscite is sometimes mistaken for another gemstone, turquoise.

Boron

Dark, slightly shiny metal

Laboratory sample of pure boron

5
B

In nature, boron is essential in small quantities for healthy plant growth. Some boron compounds are a natural antiseptic, used to heal minor wounds. This hard semimetal is used in industry to make a type of heat-resistant glass called borosilicate. Boron is also added to fiberglass to strengthen it.

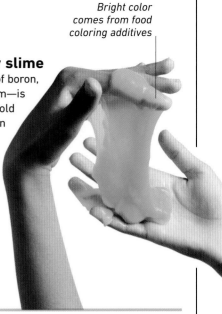

Bright color comes from food coloring additives

Ooey-gooey slime
Borax—a compound of boron, oxygen, and sodium—is a popular household cleaning chemical. It can also be used to make slime, or flubber—a rubbery play material that flows through fingers like a thick fluid but behaves like a solid when squeezed.

Keeping food fresh
As a metal, aluminum is malleable, meaning that it can be fashioned into very thin foil-like sheets. This foil is used in the packaging of food and medicines. With a thickness of just fractions of a millimeter, it provides a complete barrier to light, oxygen, moisture, and bacteria.

Heat-resistant foil

Recycling
Despite aluminum being the most widely available metal on Earth, extracting it is an expensive process. This is mainly due to the large amounts of electricity used to extract the metal from aluminum oxide, which has a high melting point. Recycling the metal is important for industry because reusing aluminum is 90 percent more energy-efficient than making new aluminum. One popular way to recycle the metal is by making soda cans, which are the world's most recycled container.

An average soda can contains about 70 percent recycled aluminum.

Transmitting electricity
Aluminum is an excellent conductor of electricity, so it is an ideal metal for use in power cables. The light weight of the aluminum cables means that fewer pylons are required to support them, reducing the cost of construction and shortening the time it takes to build networks of cables.

Aluminum fuselage is light-weight, so the plane uses less fuel to fly.

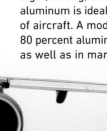

Flying metal
Light, strong, and resistant to corrosion, aluminum is ideal for use in the manufacture of aircraft. A modern plane can contain up to 80 percent aluminum—used in its pure form as well as in many high-strength alloys.

Gallium

31 Ga Similar in appearance to aluminum, gallium is a soft, silvery metal. However, unlike aluminum, this element has a much lower melting point of 84.2°F (29°C)—a cube of pure gallium will melt in your hand due to body heat. Some compounds of gallium are useful in semiconductors and are common in the electronics industry.

Needlelike crystals

Solid piece of pure gallium melting

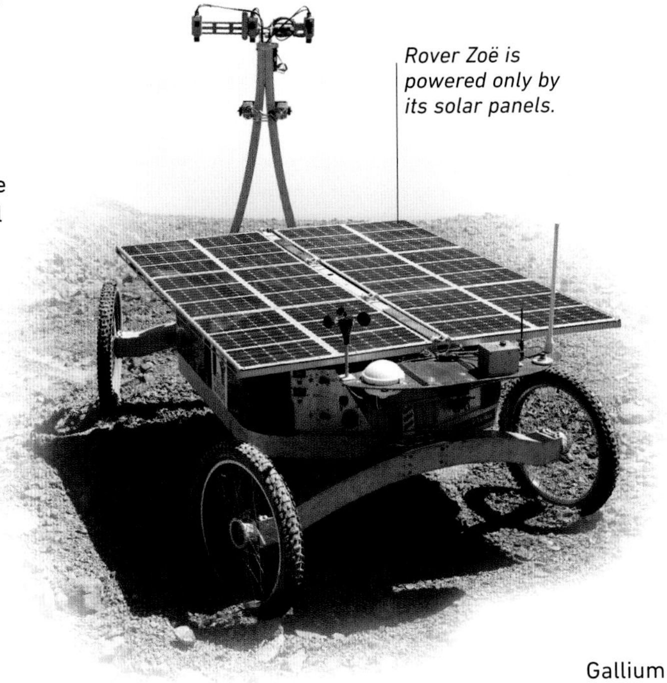

Diaspore

Minerals that contain gallium are rare, but very small amounts of it can be found in ores such as diaspore. Trace amounts of gallium are present in some other ores, including sphalerite, germanite, and bauxite.

Diaspore

Rover Zoë is powered only by its solar panels.

Searching for life

Zoë is a rover built by researchers at Carnegie Mellon University, Pennsylvania. Solar panels on the rover generate power using cells made of gallium arsenide. In 2005, this rover was used for the first time in the dry environment of South America's Atacama Desert to search for signs of microscopic life. This exercise allowed scientists to study technologies that may be useful in future rovers that explore Mars.

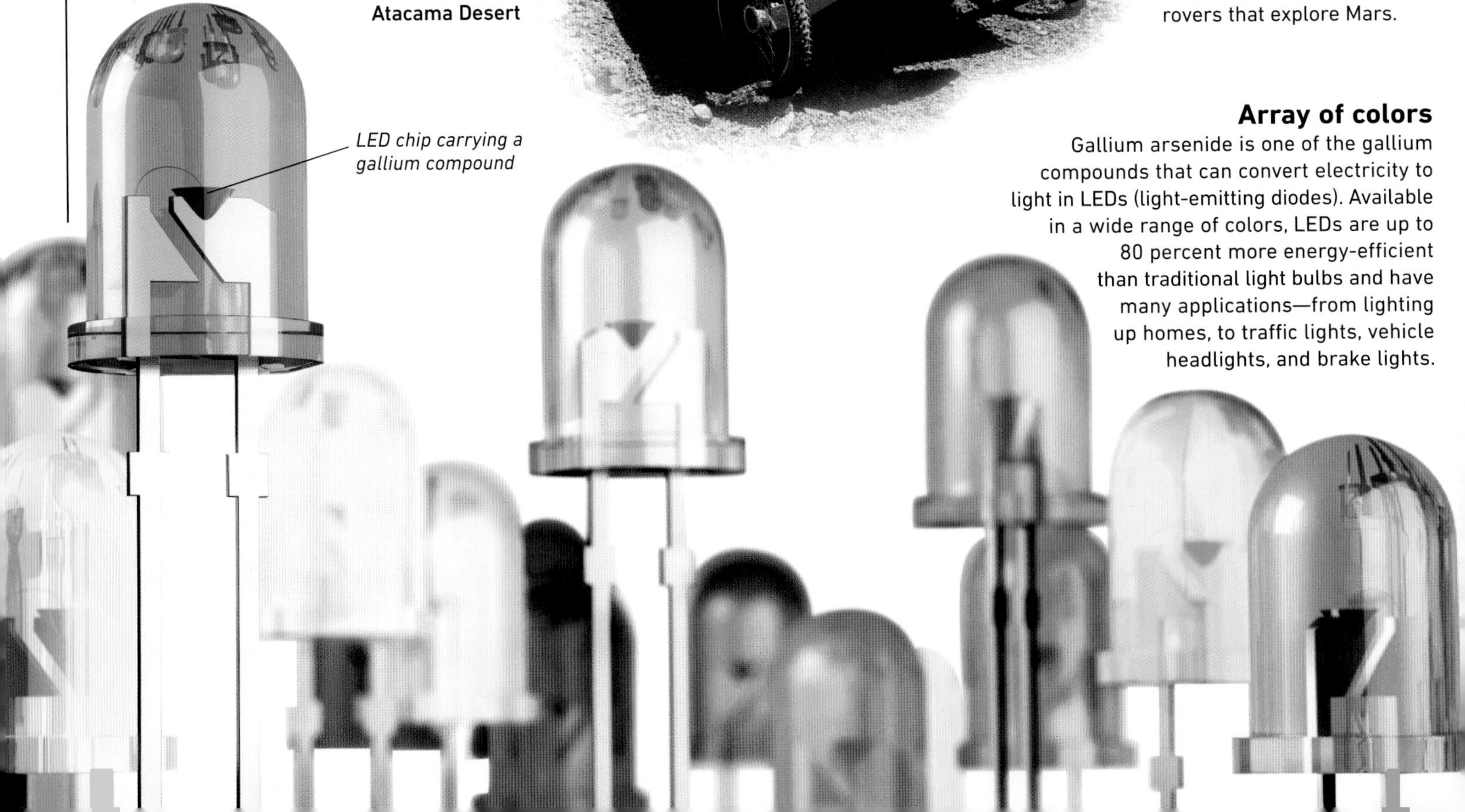

Rover Zoë in the Atacama Desert

LED chip carrying a gallium compound

Array of colors

Gallium arsenide is one of the gallium compounds that can convert electricity to light in LEDs (light-emitting diodes). Available in a wide range of colors, LEDs are up to 80 percent more energy-efficient than traditional light bulbs and have many applications—from lighting up homes, to traffic lights, vehicle headlights, and brake lights.

Indium

49 In

This element is named for the vivid indigo color that its atoms emit when electricity passes through it. Indium is generally found in nature combined with a mineral containing zinc or iron. Today, it is commonly used to make touchscreens. Like tin, it is also known as a metal that produces a shrieking noise when bent.

Pure indium mold cast in a laboratory

Indigo discovery

Indium salts, which are a type of indium compound, produce an indigo-blue color when heated strongly. German chemist Ferdinand Reich, the original discoverer of indium, was color-blind, and needed his colleague Hieronymus Richter to see the indigo line in indium's color spectrum. When Richter claimed the element's discovery for himself, the two men fell out.

Extracting indium

Traces of indium can be found in several minerals, including sphalerite, quartz, and pyrite. However, the element is often collected as a by-product in the production of zinc and copper.

Sphalerite

Making touchscreens

Indium is mainly used to make indium tin oxide, a compound present in touchscreens and solar panels. With such a huge demand for touchscreens in modern electronics—from phones to tablets—indium's scarcity is a concern.

Indigo-blue flame

Thallium

81 Tl

This toxic element's name comes from *thallos*, the Greek word for a "green shoot" or "twig"—thallium emits a vibrant green color when directly inserted into a flame. Thallium was often used as a rodent poison before many accidental deaths led to a ban on its use in the US in 1972.

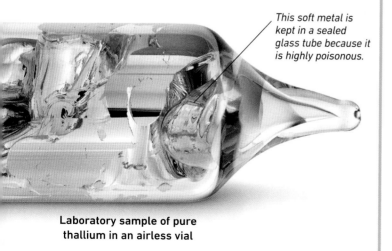

This soft metal is kept in a sealed glass tube because it is highly poisonous.

Laboratory sample of pure thallium in an airless vial

Nihonium

113 Nh

Named and placed on the periodic table in 2016, nihonium is one of the most recent additions to the table. It is named after *Nihon*, the Japanese word for "Japan," the country where the element was created. It has no known uses.

Professor Kosuke Morita, who led the team at RIKEN.

History of discovery

Nihonium was first claimed by Russian research scientists, but ultimately a team from RIKEN (The Institute of Physical and Chemical Research) in Japan were credited with the discovery of element number 113.

The Carbon Group

The six elements of the carbon group sit between the boron group and the nitrogen group.

Like its neighbors to the left and right on the periodic table, the carbon group is another mixed bag of elements. While carbon is a nonmetal, silicon and germanium are semimetals. Tin and lead are common metals that have been used in industry for centuries, while flerovium is an artificial element with no known applications other than in research.

Carbon

6 C

Element number six is arguably one of the most important of all of the 118 known elements. All organic, living things on Earth contain carbon atoms. Carbon is unique because it can form bonds with itself, and as such, it produces millions of compounds, including those important for life—amino acids, fats, oils, and DNA. From fossil fuels to diamonds, plastics, and all living organisms, carbon is everywhere.

Uncut diamond, a form of carbon

Colorless, crystalline mineral

Soft graphite

Common carbon

Graphite and diamond are two especially common forms of carbon. Their distinctive atomic structures mean they have very different properties: graphite is the soft and slippery "lead" used in pencils, and diamonds are ultra-hard precious gemstones also used as a cutting tool in industry.

Glasslike carbon

This manmade material is called glassy carbon. It has a very high resistance to heat, and does not easily react with oxygen. This means it can be used at high temperatures, for example, to make metalworking crucibles that hold molten metals.

Fossil bone analysis

Formula One racing car

Carbon dating

A radioactive form (isotope) of carbon called carbon-14 can be used to date ancient materials, such as bones. Over time, carbon-14 in an object breaks down, or "decays." By knowing how long it takes for half of the radioactive carbon atoms to decay (an object's half-life), and studying the amount of carbon-14 that remains, scientists can calculate the item's age.

Silicon

Si 14

The second-most abundant element in Earth's crust after oxygen, silicon forms the basis of many rocks. Found all over Earth, it is one of the major components of sand, in the form of its compound silicon dioxide. When separated from oxygen, silicon is a bluish-gray solid.

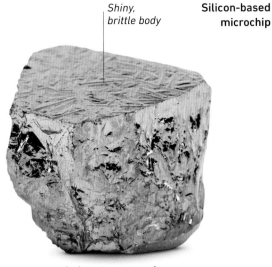

Shiny, brittle body

Laboratory sample of pure silicon

Silicon-based microchip

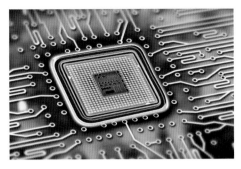

Microchips

From smartphones to missiles, modern machines need microchips to work. A microchip, which stores and processes information, is constructed from a tiny wafer of silicon—a semiconductor that controls data-rich electrical signals precisely and quickly.

Plastic bag

Plastic box

Powerful plastic

Plastic is an artificial material made up of long chains of carbon atoms. Chemists can combine other elements—such as hydrogen, oxygen, fluorine, or chlorine—with carbon, to manufacture different types of plastic for a variety of applications. Water resistant and relatively cheap, plastics are widely used in homes, from toys to toothbrushes. Plastic is also used in construction, packaging, and the making of cars.

Fossil fuels

Coal, natural gas, and oil are carbon-based fossil fuels—fuels formed in Earth's crust from the remains of ancient organisms. They form the basis of the world's energy supply, but concerns over pollution from burning them have led to the growing use of alternative energy sources.

Chimney releases pollutants

Cooling tower releases water vapor.

Light and sturdy

A lightweight, ultra-strong, manmade material called carbon fiber is used in the aerospace and automobile industries, where it can replace much heavier materials such as steel. Racing cars made of carbon fiber components are lighter and faster than earlier cars.

Tin

50
Sn

Mined since 3000 BCE, tin is combined with copper to form bronze, a strong alloy. Bronze played an important role in the development of many civilizations, allowing people to make weapons, tools, utensils, and statues. Tin is also combined with lead to make solder—a fusible alloy used to join metals together, especially in electronic devices.

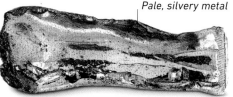

Pale, silvery metal

Laboratory sample of pure tin

Auguste Rodin's bronze sculpture "The Thinker," in Stockholm, Sweden

Bronze

Most modern bronze sculptures contain roughly 10 percent tin (the rest is copper). More resistant to rust—and harder—than iron, bronze has been an ideal material for sculptors for nearly 5,000 years. Modern applications also include propellers for ships and strings for guitars.

Tin toy train from 1900

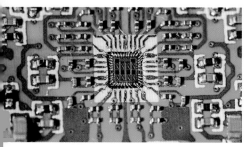

Child's play

The malleability of tin has made it useful in making toys over the last two centuries. Tin toys were often made with tinplate—a steel plate coated with a thin layer of tin. Many such toys are now collectible items.

Germanium

32
Ge

This brittle semimetal was discovered in 1886 by the German chemist Clemens Alexander Winkler, and it is named after his home country, Germany. Germanium is an important element in technology, used in the production of high-quality lenses for microscopes and cameras.

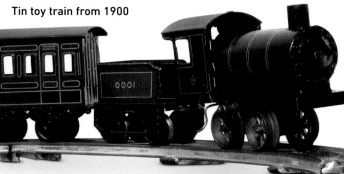

Laboratory-refined germanium disc

Computer chips

Like silicon, germanium is a semiconductor, and it is often combined with silicon to make computer chips. Seen here is a silicon-germanium chip that allows data to be transferred at very high speeds.

Flerovium

114
Fl

A synthetic element, flerovium was first produced in 1998 when scientists in Russia smashed together plutonium and calcium atoms. This highly radioactive element was given its official name in 2012, and despite it being placed in group 14 of the periodic table, some scientists thought it might act more like the noble gases in group 18.

Georgy Flyorov

Flerovium is named after the Flerov Laboratory of Nuclear Reactions in Russia, where the element was discovered. The laboratory, in turn, is named after the Russian physicist Georgy Flyorov.

Lead

82
Pb

Like tin, lead and its compounds have been used for about 5,000 years. This gray metal is soft, malleable, and resistant to rust. In the past, it was used to make many things, including coins, plumbing pipes, and paint glazes. Awareness about lead's toxicity has limited its applications today, which include car batteries, electricity cables, and decorative stained glass.

Dull gray metal

Pure lead refined in a laboratory

Shiny, green glaze

Brownish-yellow crystals containing a lead compound

Chinese earthenware model of a pigsty from Later Han Dynasty, 206 BCE–220 CE

Anglesite
This mineral contains a lead-sulfur compound that is one of the main sources of lead. Anglesite is produced in nature when oxygen reacts with galena—another ore of lead.

Lead glaze
The green glaze on this model of a pigsty from ancient China is made of lead compounds. When such a coating is applied to pottery, it makes them waterproof. Once fired in a kiln, the lead glaze becomes shiny.

Modern lead-acid car batteries are sealed and require no maintenance.

Extra sparkle
Lead crystal—a type of decorative glassware—is glass that contains at least 24 percent lead oxide, which makes it heavier. It also bends light more than regular crystal, and sparkles more as a result. Lead was used extensively in glassware before potential health risks over its use limited the manufacture of lead crystal.

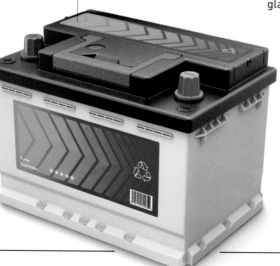

Lead power
A rechargeable car battery is sometimes called a lead-acid battery. This is because it typically contains lead plates that are coated with lead dioxide and sulfuric acid. A lead-acid battery powers a car's electrical system, including the lighting and ignition.

Lead crystal has a distinctive gray shade and a bright finish.

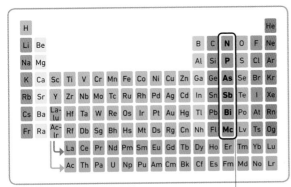

The six group 15 elements sit between the carbon and oxygen groups on the periodic table.

The Nitrogen Group

The metals, semimetals, and nonmetals in this group are known as the "pnictogens," from an ancient Greek word that means "to choke." This refers to the potential toxicity of nitrogen, the only gas in this group; the rest are solids. Phosphorus is the most reactive member, while the chemistry of moscovium, the newest addition, is largely unknown.

Nitrogen

7 N

This element makes up 78 percent of Earth's atmosphere. An invisible and odorless gas, nitrogen is continually transferred between the environment and living things in a cycle. In the soil, nitrogen plays a vital role in the growth of plants and fungi. Animals make use of nitrogen to build proteins, which are essential to life.

Seen here stored in a glass sphere, nitrogen gas gives off a purple glow when electrified.

Nitratine
A compound of sodium and nitrogen, nitratine is one of the few naturally occurring minerals that is rich in nitrogen. It is found in dry, arid areas, and is usually white or pale pink in color.

The nitrogen cycle
Nitrogen is an essential element for Earth's ecosystem. It is recycled between the atmosphere, the surface, and living things—plants, animals, fungi, and bacteria.

1. Lightning turns nitrogen in the air into nitrogen compounds, which mix in rainwater and then fall to the ground.

6. Bacteria in the soil break apart the nitrogen compounds, returning pure nitrogen into the air.

4. Animals take in the nitrogen compounds when they eat plant matter, and release it in their dung.

5. Fungi, such as mushrooms, break down the dung, which releases these compounds back into the soil.

3. The nitrogen compounds are taken up by plants.

2. Bacteria in the soil and plant roots also produce nitrogen compounds from nitrogen in the air.

Phosphorus

15 P While pure phosphorus can ignite spontaneously and inflict burns and injuries, it also plays a vital role in human biology. Like calcium, phosphorus strengthens bones and teeth. It is also present in deoxyribonucleic acid (DNA)—the chemical in our cells that carries our genetic information.

Apatite
This phosphorus-rich ore gets its name from the Greek word *apate*, which means "deceit," because apatite often resembles crystals of other minerals such as aquamarine. Its main use is in the manufacture of fertilizer, which requires phosphorus.

Taste matters
A 12-oz (350-ml) can of cola contains about 0.002 oz (60 mg) of phosphorus, in the safe form of phosphoric acid. This ingredient is widely used in soft drinks to bring out a tangy, sharp taste. It also prevents the growth of bacteria in the soda.

Glass of cola

It's a trap!
All plants need nitrogen in large quantities to grow. The Venus flytrap grows in nitrogen-poor soil, so it supplements its nitrogen requirement by feeding on insects and absorbing this element from them. It catches insects in its pressure-sensitive leaves, which shut to form a stomachlike space for trapping the prey. The trap fills with liquid chemicals that dissolve the prey, which is slowly absorbed through the leaf's surface.

Venus flytrap

Flies supply 75 percent of the nitrogen that this plant needs to survive.

Titan is shrouded in a dense, orange-brown smog that is mostly nitrogen.

Nitrogen-rich atmosphere
Saturn's largest moon, Titan, is unusual. Not only is it the only moon in the Solar System to have an atmosphere, it has one that is 98 percent nitrogen. The remaining 2 percent is mostly hydrogen and methane. Some scientists think that nitrogen may have been delivered to Titan's atmosphere by ancient comets that crashed into it.

Nitrogen-based fuel is twice as powerful as gasoline.

Fueling the race
When combined with carbon and hydrogen, nitrogen creates an immensely powerful fuel called nitromethane. This fuel generates the force that accelerates dragsters to speeds of more than 300 mph (480 km/h).

Arsenic

As 33

One of the few elements that exhibit the properties of both metals and nonmetals, arsenic is a "metalloid" or semimetal. It is found in many minerals in Earth's crust, often combined with oxygen, chlorine, or sulfur. While arsenic has a reputation as a deadly poison, it has also been used as a medicine in the past. If ingested, it accumulates in human hair and fingernails, both of which can be checked for arsenic poisoning.

Pure arsenic refined in a laboratory

As a metal, arsenic is shiny and gray.

Cluster of realgar crystals

Realgar

This arsenic sulfide mineral is found in hot volcanic springs and is an important source of arsenic. Realgar is toxic, and has been used as a rat poison and a weedkiller.

Detecting arsenic

In the early 1800s, arsenic compounds, which are tasteless and odorless, could be used to poison food or drink without being detected. In 1836, the English chemist James Marsh devised a method (shown here) of detecting even the tiniest amounts of arsenic in food. This was called the Marsh Test.

2. Arsine gas flows through this tube.

3. The gas is heated and it releases arsenic compounds.

1. Tainted food sample is mixed with zinc and sulfuric acid. If the food contains arsenic, this mixture will release arsine gas.

4. Arsenic compounds are collected here.

Volcanic vapor releases arsenic into the atmosphere.

Arsenic accumulates in the fern's leaves, forming a natural defense against predators such as grasshoppers.

Poison fern

An unusual plant known as the Chinese brake fern is able to absorb large amounts of arsenic from the soil. The toxic element arms the fern, protecting it against potential pests. In an effort to cleanse farming soil of toxins, farmers in many parts of the world are encouraged to plant the fern to soak up excess arsenic left behind in the soil by insecticides.

Explosive gases

Many minerals in Earth's crust have high concentrations of arsenic compounds and volcanic gases push these out into the atmosphere. When a volcano erupts, it releases a complicated mixture of chemicals at the surface, including a lot of arsenic. This can contaminate the air or nearby groundwater sources.

Antimony

Sb 51

This metalloid has two forms—one is a brittle, silvery metal, and the other is a nonmetallic gray powder. Antimony's symbol—Sb—is not associated with its own name, but comes from *stibium*, the Latin name for an antimony compound called antimony sulfide, used in manufacturing some types of plastic.

Ancient eye cosmetics
Compounds containing antimony have been used as black eyeliners by many civilizations. Known as kohl in some parts of the world, its use is controversial because the antimony and lead used to make it are considered to be toxic.

Painting of Egyptian Pharaoh Amenhotep I

Kohl is a dark eyeliner.

This silvery semimetal is hard but brittle.

Pure antimony crystals refined in a laboratory

A sad note
Mozart's death in 1791 at the young age of 35 has been the subject of much debate among historians. One of the popular theories is that he died as a result of accidental antimony poisoning from a medicine that he had been prescribed. This painting called *The Death Of Mozart* by Irish artist Henry O'Neill depicts the gifted composer's last moments.

Bismuth

Bi 83

A heavy metal with a low melting point, bismuth forms incredible rainbow-colored crystals. An oxide layer on the surface produces bright yellows, pinks, reds, and blues. As a result, bismuth was used widely to decorate items such as wooden chests. Bismuth was so popular in 15th-century Germany that artists using this element formed their own guild of master craftsmen.

Bismuth crystals refined in a laboratory

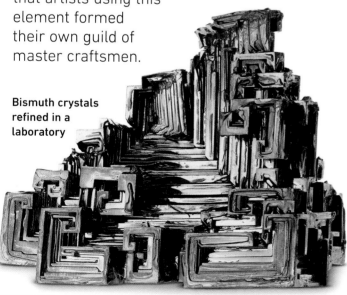

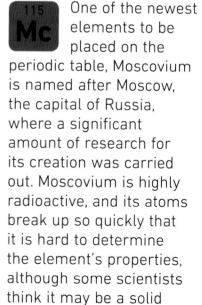

Makeup
The shiny, "pearling" effect seen in cosmetics, such as nail polish, comes from a compound called bismuth oxychloride. When hit by light, its crystals produce a pearly sheen. This compound has been used in cosmetics since ancient Egyptian times.

Moscovium

Mc 115

One of the newest elements to be placed on the periodic table, Moscovium is named after Moscow, the capital of Russia, where a significant amount of research for its creation was carried out. Moscovium is highly radioactive, and its atoms break up so quickly that it is hard to determine the element's properties, although some scientists think it may be a solid metal. Currently, it has no known applications.

All six elements of this group are able to form compounds with each other.

The Oxygen Group

These elements are sometimes called "chalcogens," from the Greek word *chalcos*, meaning "ore formers." Ores of most metals are compounds of either oxygen or sulfur, both of which belong to this group. While oxygen is a gas, the other members are solids at room temperature. Oxygen and sulfur are nonmetals; selenium, tellurium, and polonium are semimetals. The artificial element, livermorium, is largely unknown—only a few atoms have been made.

Oxygen

8 O

The third most abundant element in the Universe, oxygen makes up 21 percent of the air we breathe. This colorless gas becomes a blue liquid at −297°F (−183°C), which is used in the medical industry to preserve tissue samples. Oxygen has several forms, including ozone, which forms a protective barrier between Earth and the damaging ultraviolet rays of the Sun.

This glass sphere stores pure oxygen, which produces a silver-blue glow when electrified.

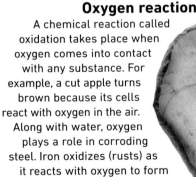

Oxygen reaction

A chemical reaction called oxidation takes place when oxygen comes into contact with any substance. For example, a cut apple turns brown because its cells react with oxygen in the air. Along with water, oxygen plays a role in corroding steel. Iron oxidizes (rusts) as it reacts with oxygen to form orange-red iron oxide that flakes away, weakening the metal.

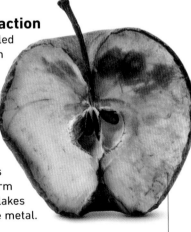

This apple's brown flesh is a sign of oxidation.

Oxygen cycle

All living beings depend on oxygen for their existence. Animals on land and in water breathe in oxygen as they respire. However, while animals breathe out carbon dioxide in this process, plants take in carbon dioxide. Then, plants combine it with sunlight and water to produce energy and release oxygen back into the atmosphere in a process called photosynthesis.

Specialized masks connected to oxygen tanks provide oxygen to the mountaineer.

Carl Wilhelm Scheele   **Joseph Priestley**

Disputed history

In the time before email and social media, most messages were sent slowly by hand. This sometimes led to disagreements over who first discovered an element. Oxygen is one of many elements with a disputed history of discovery. The German-Swedish chemist Carl Wilhelm Scheele first identified oxygen, but the English chemist Joseph Priestly was first to publish his results of finding the gas, so he is often credited with its discovery.

Thin air

At high altitudes, such as on top of mountains, the air is thinner than it is at sea level. This means that the oxygen gas present is more spread out, which makes it difficult to breathe. Mountaineers, therefore, often carry a supply of oxygen in tanks.

The green color is produced by oxygen located up to 60 miles (95 km) above Earth's surface.

Wood needs oxygen to burn, releasing heat and light.

Burning up

When something burns, it is said to be undergoing a reaction called combustion. This process involves three things: oxygen, a fuel (such as wood), and the release of heat (such as fire). If the supply of oxygen is removed, the fire will be extinguished.

Colorful sky

The northern lights—a naturally occurring display of light in some arctic regions—are the result of particles from the Sun colliding with gases in Earth's atmosphere. Oxygen and nitrogen in the air are the gases responsible for the dazzling colors. The green color is produced when the Sun's particles collide with oxygen, while the blue and violet colors are produced as a result of their collision with nitrogen. Canada, northern Europe, and Iceland are some of the places where the northern lights are most visible.

Selenium

Se 34

This semimetal has two pure forms—one is powdery and red and the other is a hard, gray metal. As well as being used to modify glass, selenium is used to coat solar cells. Its compounds are found in many everyday products, from dandruff shampoos to photocopiers.

Metallic sheen on gray selenium

Chunk of pure gray selenium refined in a laboratory

Red color due to a selenium glaze

A touch of color
Certain selenium compounds can change the color of glass—some can provide an orange-red tint; others make the glass colorless. Bright ruby reds or pink hues in glass are often due to the addition of selenium.

Tellurium

Te 52

Rare in Earth's crust, tellurium is named after *tellus*, the Latin name for "Earth." Like selenium, it is a toxic semimetal with a pungent, garliclike smell. It has several uses in industry, including in the manufacture of fiberoptic cables and semiconductors.

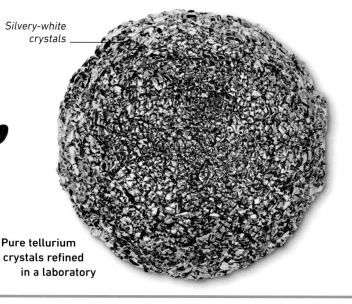

Silvery-white crystals

Pure tellurium crystals refined in a laboratory

Sulfur

S 16

Once believed to be an important ingredient in the making of the Philosopher's Stone—a legendary substance capable of turning common metals into gold—sulfur was used widely by early alchemists. In its raw form, this nonmetal is found as yellow crystals, and is renowned for its foul odor. Sulfur also keeps the body healthy, from helping resist harmful bacteria to aiding in the growth of muscles. In industry, it is used to make a chemical called sulfuric acid.

Laboratory sample of pure sulfur granules

Celestine
Available throughout Earth in its raw form, sulfur also appears in many compounds. The sulfur compound strontium sulfate is present in celestine, a pale blue crystalline mineral.

In my defense
When faced by a predator, a skunk turns its back and sprays a combination of smelly sulfur compounds at its enemy. These compounds are called thiols and are related to alcohols. Not only do they smell foul, they can also irritate the victim's eyes and lungs.

Powdery yellow sulfur deposits

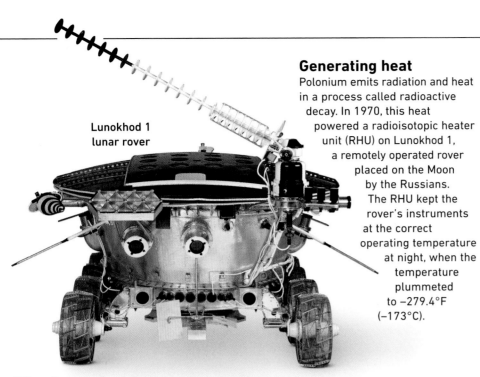

Lunokhod 1
lunar rover

Generating heat
Polonium emits radiation and heat in a process called radioactive decay. In 1970, this heat powered a radioisotopic heater unit (RHU) on Lunokhod 1, a remotely operated rover placed on the Moon by the Russians. The RHU kept the rover's instruments at the correct operating temperature at night, when the temperature plummeted to −279.4°F (−173°C).

Livermorium

116 Lv Named in 2012, livermorium is an artificial, super-heavy element that was made by colliding curium and calcium atoms in a machine called a particle accelerator. It was discovered in partnership by Russian scientists at the Joint Institute for Nuclear Research (JINR) in Dubna, Russia, and American scientists at the Lawrence Livermore National Laboratory in California. Livermorium is named after this American laboratory. With only a few atoms ever produced, this element has no known uses outside of research.

Polonium

84 Po This element was named after Poland, the country of birth of Marie Curie—the chemist who discovered polonium. This silvery-gray semimetal is highly radioactive, and that property has been harnessed to provide heat in space probes. It is also used in scientific research.

Sulfur springs
Volcanic hot springs are often a natural source of sulfur. The hot water in the springs is produced as a result of volcanic activity underground and, as the water reaches the surface, it brings dissolved sulfur minerals with it. At this hot spring near the Dallol Volcano in Ethiopia, water containing natural sulfur and minerals has dried up, leaving behind a yellow crust.

Acid rain
Burning fossil fuels, such as coal, releases sulfur and nitrogen compounds into the air. These react with the oxygen and water in the atmosphere to form acids, which then fall to the ground as rain. This acid rain can dissolve stone that is exposed to the weather. Statues and buildings made from limestone and marble are most vulnerable to acid rain corrosion.

Vulcanization
Adding sulfur to rubber hardens the rubber and makes it flexible and more durable. This process is called vulcanization. Vulcanized rubber is up to 10 times stronger than natural rubber. Vehicle tires, bowling balls, and rubber hoses are all made of vulcanized rubber.

Corroded limestone statue of King Charles II in Lichfield Cathedral, Staffordshire, UK

Hot springs in the Danakil Depression, Ethiopia

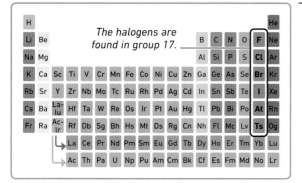

The halogens are found in group 17.

Halogens

The word halogen means "salt forming." Elements in this group are able to create salts when they react with metals. For example, lithium bromide is a compound of the halogen bromine and the metal lithium, while table salt—sodium chloride—is a compound of chlorine and sodium. The first four members of this group—fluorine, chlorine, bromine, and iodine—are all very reactive in nature. Astatine is far less reactive, while the chemistry of tennessine—a halogen confirmed in 2016—is still a mystery.

Chlorine

17 Cl

This halogen has a useful and a dangerous side—while it is a crucial component in water purification, it is also a toxic gas. As a pure element, it has limited applications, such as in disinfectants for swimming pools. However, chlorine is present in compounds used for a whole host of industrial processes, including those that produce medicines.

Cube-shaped crystals

Common salt
Before it is purified and placed at the dinner table, table salt can be found as a crystalline mineral in its natural form. Known commonly as rock salt, its scientific name is sodium chloride.

This tube shows the level of chlorine in the water. The darker the sample, the more chlorine in the pool.

This tube indicates the pH of the water. The more yellow the sample, the lower the pH value and the greater the acidity.

Halite
Chlorine can be extracted from the mineral halite using a process called electrolysis. Dissolving halite in water and passing electricity through it releases chlorine gas. Huge amounts of chlorine can also be found in the oceans, meaning an almost limitless supply is available naturally on Earth.

Purifying water
Chemicals containing chlorine are used to disinfect water in swimming pools. The chlorine helps to kill bacteria and to keep the water's acidity at the correct level. The acidity is measured using the pH scale, which ranges from 0 to14. A pH in the middle—about 7.4–7.6—is ideal. If it is too high or low, the water can damage skin and irritate eyes.

Fluorine

F ⁹ The most reactive of all halogens, fluorine has a reputation as a dangerously unstable element. It reacts violently with metals, hydrogen gas, and water, and will even react with some noble gases, which are normally inert.

Fluoride

Some fluorine compounds play a vital role in oral health. When added to toothpastes and the water supply in the form of safe fluorides, these compounds help prevent tooth decay by strengthening tooth enamel.

Fluorite

Fluorite crystals

Also known as fluorspar, fluorite is a naturally occurring mineral consisting mainly of the compound calcium fluoride. When fluorite reacts with sulfuric acid, it produces hydrogen fluoride, which is the main source of fluorine in industry.

Green color is due to impurities in the crystal.

Deadly pesticide

In the 1940s and 1950s, the chlorine-based chemical DDT (dichloro-diphenyl-trichloroethane) was used widely as a pesticide to curb insect-borne diseases. However, concerns about its impact on wildlife and human health grew until it was banned in the US in 1972. Today, it is banned in most countries and severely restricted in others, where it is used mainly to fight outbreaks of malaria, a deadly disease spread by mosquitoes.

Néocide DDT
la terreur des moustiques

This poster from the 1950s shows an elephant spraying a can of DDT to kill mosquitoes.

These strong pipes—for use in house construction—are composed of PVC.

An indispensable plastic

Arguably one of the most important compounds to contain chlorine is polyvinylchloride (PVC). This type of plastic has a huge number of uses in and around the home, including water pipes, garden furniture, and waterproof clothing.

British World War II gas mask

Filter unit absorbs deadly chlorine gas.

Gas warfare

A pungent, yellow-green gas, chlorine affects the eyes, nose, throat, and lungs, by causing a choking and irritating effect that can lead to suffocation. As such, chlorine was first used as a chemical weapon in World War I, which led to the development of gas masks for troops. By World War II, gas masks were provided for troops and civilians alike.

Chlorine-based bleach

Bleaching agent

Paper products such as napkins, tissues, and printer paper can be made bright white by using chlorine as a bleaching agent. Common household bleach, which is used to kill germs, contains a powerful chlorine compound called sodium hypochlorite.

Bromine

35 Br

The third member of the halogen family, bromine is a distinct red-brown liquid. It is one of only two elements on the periodic table that are liquid at room temperature, the other being mercury. Toxic in nature, bromine must be handled with care. Its name comes from the Greek word *bromos* meaning "stench"—a reference to its unpleasant smell.

Bromine vapor

A drop of liquid bromine formed at room temperature

Pure bromine stored in a glass sphere

Medicinal salt
Potassium bromide, a compound similar to common table salt, was used in the late 19th century to help patients sleep. Today, it is useful in veterinary medicine for controlling seizures in dogs.

White, saltlike crystals

Cloth dyed with Tyrian purple

Bromine purple
Tyrian purple is a naturally occurring dye secreted by some sea snails. It contains a bromine-based compound. In Ancient Rome, this dye was highly prized, and purple clothing was seen as a sign of great wealth and importance.

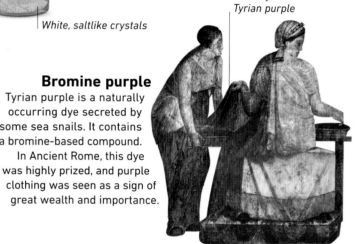

Fresco at the Villa of the Mysteries in the ancient Roman city of Pompeii, Italy

Take a picture
Due to its light sensitivity, the compound silver bromide is put to good use in black-and-white photography. Photographic film coated with a silver bromide solution changes color when exposed to light. This creates an image that is developed into a photograph.

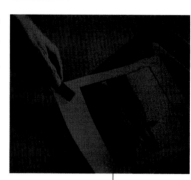

The image darkens on exposure to light.

Muride
The French chemist Antoine-Jérôme Balard discovered bromine and originally named it muride. This was based on *muria*, a Latin word for "brine," because Balard had extracted the element from seawater. This name was later changed to "bromine" to match the other halogens known at the time.

The Dead Sea in the Middle East contains high quantities of bromine.

Iodine

53 I

The name iodine comes from the Greek word *iodes*, which means "violet." When heated, this halogen changes directly from a solid to a violet vapor without turning into a liquid—a process called sublimation. Iodine is important in our diet because it is vital to the production of chemicals that regulate body functions, including growth.

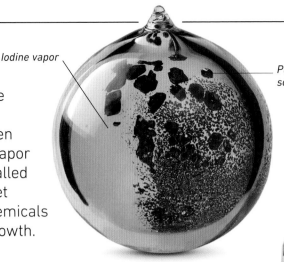

Iodine vapor

Purple-black solid iodine

Pure iodine stored in a glass sphere

Polarized surface provides extra protection against the Sun's ultraviolet radiation.

Seaweed diet
Most seaweed contains a large amount of iodine. The Japanese consume a lot of iodine, as a traditional Japanese diet will often feature seaweed.

Protective eyewear
Polarized sunglasses are covered with a thin plastic film dipped in an iodine solution. This coating reduces the Sun's harsh glare. Many skiers use polarized glasses because sunlight reflecting off white snow can make it hard to see.

Astatine

85 At

A highly radioactive element, astatine is also very rare. There is an estimated amount of less than 1 oz (30 g) present in Earth's crust. In 1940, Italian-American physicist Emilio Gino Segrè shared the discovery of this element with American physicists Dale R. Corson and Kenneth Ross MacKenzie.

Emilio Gino Segrè
In addition to his discovery of astatine, Segrè is also credited with discovering the element technetium. He won the 1959 Nobel Prize in Physics for his discovery of the antiproton—a particle with the same mass as a proton but with a negative electric charge.

Tennessine

117 Ts

In November 2016, element 117 was named Tennessine as a tribute to the state of Tennessee. This region is home to the Oak Ridge National Laboratory, which played a prominent role in the research that led to the discovery of this element.

A nuclear reactor at the Oak Ridge National Laboratory, Tennessee

Researchers use a crane to move fuel rods into the reactor.

The noble gases sit in group 18—the final group of the periodic table.

This sample of helium is stored in a glass sphere.

Helium is a colorless gas, but it glows purple when electrified.

Noble Gases

Because they are colorless, odorless, tasteless, and mostly unreactive, the noble gases were not easy to identify. But once one was found, the rest followed fairly quickly. Argon was the first of the family to be discovered, by British chemists Morris William Travers and William Ramsay in 1894. With the subsequent discoveries of helium, krypton, neon, and xenon, a whole new group on the periodic table was established.

Helium

Although abundant in the Universe, helium is not widespread on Earth. The Sun and other stars contain a lot of helium, produced by pairs of hydrogen atoms crashing into one another to make helium atoms while releasing massive amounts of energy. On Earth, helium is produced naturally as a result of radioactive decay.

Keeping cool

In a particle accelerator (a machine that smashes atoms together in scientific experiments), liquid helium is injected into the electromagnets to keep the magnets cool. The Large Hadron Collider (LHC) at CERN— the European Organization for Nuclear Research on the French-Swiss border—is the world's biggest particle accelerator. It is inside a circular underground tunnel that runs for 17 miles (27 km).

In the LHC, liquid helium cools the electromagnets to -456.3°F (-271.3°C).

Extreme-helium stars

Unlike most stars, composed primarily of hydrogen, extreme-helium stars such as Wolf-Rayet 124 (left) are made up of approximately 85 percent helium. Wolf-Rayet 124 is an ultra massive star surrounded by the intensely hot M1-67 Nebula. This type of star also contains smaller amounts of other elements, including carbon, nitrogen, oxygen, aluminum, iron, chromium, and nickel.

Wolf-Rayet 124 glows inside the M1-67 Nebula.

Neon

This sample of neon is stored in a glass sphere. Normally a colorless gas, it gives off a red-orange glow when electrified.

Ne Perhaps the most well known of all nobles gases for its role in neon signs, neon is an unreactive element. Like helium, this transparent gas is commonly found throughout the Universe but is rare on Earth. Unlike helium, which is found mixed in natural gas, neon is available only in air. It is extracted by cooling air until it becomes a liquid. In industry, neon is used as a coolant, as well as in making some types of fluorescent lamps and in diving equipment.

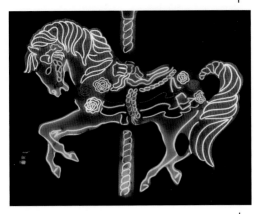

Neon lights
Gas tubes filled with neon are commonly used in bright red signs and lights. The other colors are not actually neon, but other elements; for example helium (yellow), argon (purple), and mercury (blue).

A helium–neon laser beam appears red in color.

Scanning codes
Barcodes may look like nothing more than a collection of black-and-white parallel lines, but they store data about the product that can only be read by machines. Barcode scanners use lasers made of a combination of helium and neon. These efficient lasers use very little energy, and are used in supermarkets and retail shops throughout the world.

Weather balloons collect wind data, including temperature and speed, as well as atmospheric pressure readings at high altitudes.

Up, up, and away
Helium has been used in all types of balloons, including weather balloons and party balloons. Since helium gas is lighter than air, balloons filled with this element float upward in the atmosphere. Unlike hydrogen, helium is not flammable, making it a much safer choice.

Argon

Ar 18

This element's name comes from *argos*, the Greek word for "idle." True to its name, this gas does not react with any other element, so it is used when industrial processes need a stable, environment. It does not conduct heat well either, so it is often used as a filler to slow down heat loss in double-glazed windows, and to protect the rubber in car tires.

Argon gives off a pale purple color when it is electrified.

Pure argon in a glass sphere

Fighting fire
Argon extinguishers are highly recommended for suppressing electrical fires. The gas does not damage expensive equipment by leaving a residue, making it a popular choice for fire extinguishers in server and data rooms, museums, archives, and laboratories.

ARGON
UN 1006

NET WEIGHT
25 KG

The blue argon laser targets the retina during eye surgery.

Noninvasive surgery
Laser surgical procedures do not make incisions and, consequently, the affected area heals quickly. In the case of eye surgery, this blue argon laser can be used for a wide range of delicate operations on the retina.

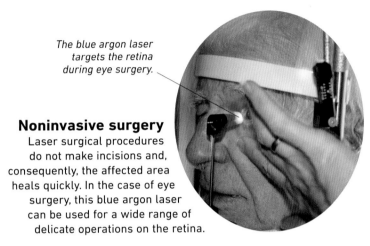

Krypton

Kr 36

A odorless and colorless gas, *krypton* means "the hidden one" in Greek. It plays an important role in airport safety—the flashing lights on most modern airport runways are filled with this gas. A krypton-filled light bulb gives off a bright white light, making it a good light source in high-speed photography.

Krypton-powered airport runway lights

Oganesson

Og 118

Only a few atoms of this highly radioactive element have been made in a laboratory. As such, not much is known about it. While scientists think it could be solid at room temperature, there is a chance that oganesson may be an inert noble gas. Discovered by a group of Russian and American scientists in Dubna, Russia, the element is named after Yuri Oganessian, the leader of the team.

Russian scientist Yuri Oganessian

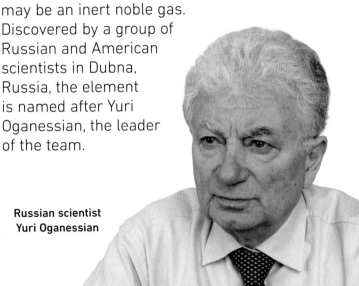

Xenon

Like most members of its group, xenon is also an unreactive, colorless, and odorless element. However, it glows a striking blue when a high voltage is applied to it, and this property makes it a valuable ingredient in car headlights and studio lights. Some rocket engines use xenon-based thrusters to propel the spacecraft forward.

Pure xenon electrified in a glass sphere

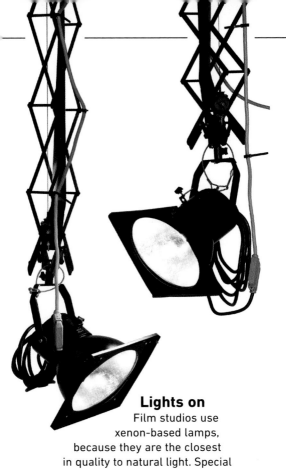

Lights on
Film studios use xenon-based lamps, because they are the closest in quality to natural light. Special effects artists use this type of light source to create an intense, straight beam of light on film sets.

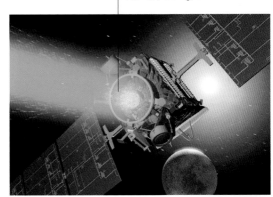

The Dawn *spacecraft carried 937 lb (425 kg) of xenon at launch.*

Rocket fuel
Xenon is used as a fuel in some rocket engines. Chemically inert and easily stored in a compact form, its atoms are heavy, so they provide more thrust compared to other fuels.

Artist's impression of NASA's *Dawn* spacecraft

Radon

Produced by the breakdown of uranium and other radioactive elements, radon is the only natural radioactive noble gas. In most places, this element exists in tiny amounts in the air, yet it is still responsible for most of the radiation on Earth. The level of radon spikes, however, around volcanic springs and geothermal power plants—power stations that use energy from volcanic rocks to generate electricity.

Radioactive materials in this mineral break down to emit radon gas.

Uraninite

Glass sphere containing radon and air

The water from this volcanic hot spring contains radon.

Hot spring baths
Radon escapes from volcanic hot springs and muds along with other gases, such as carbon dioxide and sulfur dioxide. While radon is considered to be toxic by environmental agencies, some health-seekers visit thermal baths for a dip in these waters.

Radon residue

Glossary

ACID
A corrosive substance that reacts with a base (*see* base) to form a salt and water.

ALCHEMY
Practices in medieval times that tried to turn common metals, such as lead, into gold.

ALKALI
A soluble base (*see* base).

ALLOY
A mixture of two or more metals.

ATMOSPHERIC PRESSURE
The pressure created by the gases surrounding Earth.

ATOM
The smallest unit of an element.

ATOMIC MASS
The mass of an atom measured in atomic mass units (AMU).

BASE
A corrosive substance that will react with an acid (see acid) to form a salt and water.

BLOCK
Larger sets of elements on the periodic table that may have similar properties.

BOND
The attraction between atoms that holds them together in an element or a compound.

CATALYST
A substance that can be added to a chemical reaction to speed it up.

COMBUSTION
A chemical reaction in which a fuel burns in the presence of oxygen.

COMPOUND
A substance made up of elements bonded together.

CONDUCTIVITY
The ability of a substance to let electricity, sound, or heat pass through it.

CORROSION
The process of a metal breaking down by chemically reacting with substances in the environment. An example of this is the rusting of iron through reactions with oxygen and water.

Saxophone made of bronze, a copper-tin alloy

CYCLOTRON
A type of particle accelerator. Particle accelerators are machines used to smash atoms into one another at incredibly high speeds.

ELECTROLYSIS
A technique that uses electricity to break salt compounds down into simpler substances.

ELECTRON
A negatively charged particle that orbits the nucleus of an atom.

ELEMENT
A substance that cannot be broken down into anything simpler.

EMISSION
The process of giving off light, heat, radiation, or particles.

FISSION
The process of splitting the nucleus of an atom into smaller fragments.

FOSSIL FUEL
A substance formed in Earth's crust from the remains of ancient organisms. Humans use this as fuel.

FUEL CELL
A device that converts chemical energy into electricity.

GALVANIZATION
The process of electrically coating steel with zinc to protect it from corrosion.

GENETICS
The study of inherited traits between different organisms.

GROUP
A vertical column of elements on the periodic table, with elements that often have similar properties.

HALF-LIFE
The time taken for half of the nuclei in a radioactive sample to undergo decay (*see* nuclear decay).

INERT
A way of describing a substance that does not easily undergo a chemical reaction.

INSULATOR
A substance that does not let electricity, sound, or heat flow through it easily.

ION
A charged particle produced when an atom either loses or gains electrons.

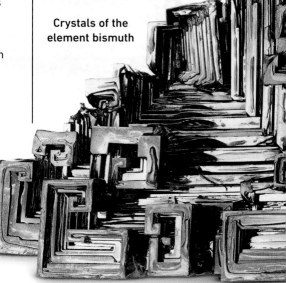

Crystals of the element bismuth

ISOTOPE
A form of an element with atoms that have the same number of protons but a different number of neutrons.

MALLEABILITY
A metal's ability to be reshaped.

MELTING POINT
The temperature at which a solid gets hot enough to turn into a liquid.

METAL
An element that is usually found as a shiny solid and is a good conductor of electricity and heat.

MINERAL
A naturally occurring form of a chemical compound, usually found in Earth's crust.

MOLECULE
A group of atoms that are chemically bonded to one another.

NEUTRON
A neutral subatomic particle found in the nucleus of an atom.

NUCLEAR BOMB
An explosive device that releases large amounts of energy and can cause mass devastation.

Rust on motorbike, an example of corrosion

NUCLEAR DECAY
A natural process in which the nuclei of radioactive atoms break down or rearrange themselves to form new nuclei.

NUCLEAR REACTOR
A device used to carry out a controlled nuclear reaction.

NUCLEUS
The dense center of an atom where protons and neutrons are found.

OPTICAL CLOCK
A special type of clock that uses light and single atoms to keep highly accurate time.

ORBITAL
Spherical layer, or shell, around the nucleus of an atom where electrons can be found.

ORE
Naturally occurring rock from which useful minerals can be extracted.

ORGANIC CHEMISTRY
A branch of chemistry that deals with the chemistry of carbon and its compounds.

OXIDE
A compound that forms when an element combines with oxygen.

PERIOD
A horizontal row of elements on the periodic table, with elements that often have very different properties.

pH SCALE
A numeric scale used to describe the acidic or basic properties of a substance. Less than 7 on the scale is described as acidic, above 7 as basic, and 7 as neutral.

PHOTOSYNTHESIS
Naturally occurring chemical reaction that plants use to turn light energy into chemical energy.

POROUS
A material with tiny holes through which liquids can pass.

PROTON
A positively charged particle in the nucleus of an atom.

RADIATION
Energy released, usually in the form of waves or particles.

RADIOACTIVITY
A process that occurs when an atom is unstable, because the protons and neutrons in the nucleus do not stick together.

Fluorite, a mineral containing fluorine

REACTIVITY
A substance's tendency to undergo chemical reactions.

SALT
A compound that forms when an acid reacts with an alkali. Sodium chloride is the most familiar example of a salt.

SEMICONDUCTOR
A material that conducts electricity better than an insulator but not as well as a metal.

SEMIMETAL
An element that displays the properties of both metals and nonmetals. It is also called a metalloid.

SOLUBLE
Dissolves in a solvent (usually water).

STATES OF MATTER
The three common states of matter are solid, liquid, or gas. In solids, particles are bound to each other, so they remain in fixed positions. In liquids, particles are loosely attached to each other, and move freely. In gases, particles are not attached to each other, and can move away.

SUBATOMIC PARTICLE
A particle that makes up an atom. These include protons, neutrons, and electrons.

SUPERALLOY
A combination of metals that can withstand extreme temperature and pressure.

SUPER-HEAVY ELEMENTS
Elements with the atomic number 104 or higher.

SYNTHETIC ELEMENT
An element created artificially in a laboratory.

Pellets of radioactive californium

TEMPERATURE
How hot or cold something is as measured on a defined scale.

TOXICITY
A measure of the poisonous properties of a substance.

TRANSURANIUM ELEMENTS
Elements with an atomic number higher than that of uranium (92).

ULTRAVIOLET RAYS
Invisible electromagnetic radiation with very short wavelengths. It is called ultraviolet because it is beyond the violet end of visible light on the electromagnetic spectrum.

VAPOR
A gas that can easily be changed back to a liquid by cooling it or putting it under pressure.

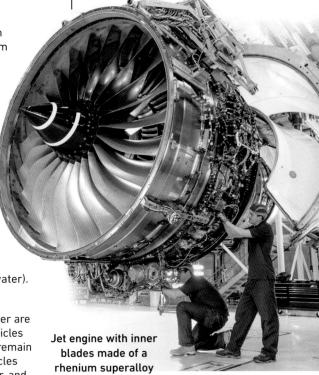

Jet engine with inner blades made of a rhenium superalloy

VERDIGRIS
A gray-green layer that forms on copper when it is exposed to air.

VOLTAGE
The force that pushes an electric current around a circuit.

WIRELESS
Transmitting messages through electromagnetic waves rather than wires.

X-RAY
A type of powerful electromagnetic radiation. X-rays can pass right through human tissue but not bone, and are used in medical science to take internal pictures of the human body.

Index

Acknowledgments

Dorling Kindersley would like to thank:
Elizabeth Wise for indexing; Caroline Stamps for proofreading; Rajesh Singh Adhikari for color corrections; and Nishwan Rasool for additional picture research.

The publisher would like to thank the following for their kind permission to reproduce their photographs:
(Key: a-above; b-below/bottom; c-center; f-far; l-left; r-right; t-top)

1 Dorling Kindersley: Ruth Jenkinson / RGB Research Limited. 2 123RF.com: David Barnard (clb). Dorling Kindersley: Ruth Jenkinson / RGB Research Limited (tl, bl, cra). Dreamstime.com: Yehuda Bernstein (tr). Getty Images: Viviane Ponti (br). 4 Alamy Stock Photo: The Granger Collection (tc). Dorling Kindersley: Ruth Jenkinson / RGB Research Limited (clb, br). 5 Dorling Kindersley: Ruth Jenkinson / RGB Research Limited (bl). 7 123RF.com: Kubais (br). Alamy Stock Photo: Science History Images (cra). 9 Dorling Kindersley: The Granger Collection (bc). 10 Dorling Kindersley: Ruth Jenkinson / RGB Research Limited (cl, c, cr, bl, bc, br). 11 Dorling Kindersley: Ruth Jenkinson / RGB Research Limited (ca, ca, cr, bl, bc, br). 12 123RF.com: Utima (br); Reinhold Wittich (cr). Dorling Kindersley: Ruth Jenkinson / RGB Research Limited (bl). 13 Alamy Stock Photo: PjrStamps (c); VintageCorner (br). Getty Images: Gamma-Rapho / Tatsuyuki TAYAMA (c). 14 123RF.com: Ramon Espelt Gorgozo (br). Dorling Kindersley: Ruth Jenkinson / RGB Research Limited (cl). 15 Depositphotos Inc: Gnomeandi (br). Dorling Kindersley: Ruth Jenkinson / RGB Research Limited (tl). 16 123RF.com: Belchonock (cl); karandaev (fcl); Kostic Dusan (bl). Alamy Stock Photo: Siim Sepp (ca). Dorling Kindersley: Ruth Jenkinson / RGB Research Limited (tc). 500px/ Marc Lapointe (crb). 17 Alamy Stock Photo: David Leone Ganado (tr); Newscom (bc). Dorling Kindersley: Ruth Jenkinson / RGB Research Limited (cla, clb, bl). 18 Dorling Kindersley: Ruth Jenkinson / Holts Gems (cl). NASA: MSFC / David Higginbotham (br). 19 123RF.com: Georgios Kollidas (bl); Sergij Popov (br). Dorling Kindersley: Ruth Jenkinson / RGB Research Limited (cla). Science Photo Library: GIPhotoStock (cr). 20 123RF.com: Steve Carroll (cr); Ben Gingell (bl). Dorling Kindersley: Ruth Jenkinson / RGB Research Limited (cl). Dreamstime.com: Yehuda Bernstein (t). 21 Alamy Stock Photo: US Marines Photo (cl). Dorling Kindersley: Ruth Jenkinson / RGB Research Limited (bl). Getty Images: Print Collector / Oxford Science Archive (br). Science Photo Library: Biophoto Associates (cra); J. C. Revy (bc). 22 Alamy

Stock Photo: Shooterstack (cra). Dorling Kindersley: Ruth Jenkinson / RGB Research Limited (bl). Getty Images: Barcroft Media / Jefta Images (bc). 23 123RF.com: Hapelena (bc). Alamy Stock Photo: Oleksiy Maksymenko (br). Dorling Kindersley: Ruth Jenkinson / RGB Research Limited (cla). 500px/ Maciej Sznek (tr). 24 123RF.com: Ruslan Gilmanshin (cb). Dorling Kindersley: Ruth Jenkinson / RGB Research Limited (cla). Dreamstime.com: Nexus7 (cra). Getty Images: Viviane Ponti (br). Rex Shutterstock: Glasshouse Images (tc). 25 Alamy Stock Photo: H.S. Photos (ca); Margo Harrison (cra). Dorling Kindersley: Ruth Jenkinson / RGB Research Limited (crb). Dreamstime.com: Radlovskyaroslav (br); Nicolas-Alain Petit (bl, clb). 26 123RF.com: David Barnard (cla); Koosen (bl); Sandra van der Steen (ca); Chris Elwell (bc). Dorling Kindersley: Ruth Jenkinson / RGB Research Limited (tc, crb). Dreamstime.com: Stockshooter (cra). 27 Alamy Stock Photo: Susan E. Degginger (br). Dorling Kindersley: Ruth Jenkinson / RGB Research Limited (tc, tr); Gary Ombler / The Tank Museum, Bovington (br). SuperStock: Age fotostock / Humbert (ca); Age fotostock / Phil Robinson (cra). 28 123RF.com: Nerthuz (ca). Dorling Kindersley: Ruth Jenkinson / RGB Research Limited (tc, bl, crb). Practicon www.practicon.com (br). 29 Dakota Matrix Minerals, photo by Tom Loomis (cla). Dorling Kindersley: Ruth Jenkinson / RGB Research Limited (tl, cb). Getty Images: Deniztuyel (bl). Science Photo Library: (cra). 30 Alamy Stock Photo: Ableimages (cla); Dembinsky Photo Associates / Mark A Schneider (tr). Dorling Kindersley: Ruth Jenkinson / RGB Research Limited (cb). 31 123RF.com: Mishoo (tr); Anton Starikov (tl). Dorling Kindersley: Ruth Jenkinson / RGB Research Limited (cb). Getty Images: De Agostini / DEA / R. Appiani (cla). © Rolls-Royce plc: (bc). Science Photo Library: Detlev van Ravenswaay (cra); Dirk Wiersma (cra). 32 Dorling Kindersley: Ruth Jenkinson / RGB Research Limited (bl); Natural History Museum, London / Tim Parmenter (tl). Dreamstime.com: Maloy40 (cla). Science Photo Library: Gary Brown (cra). 33 123RF.com: Boris Stroujko (br). Dorling Kindersley: Ruth Jenkinson / RGB Research Limited (br). NASA: Getty Images: Numismatica Ars Classica NAC AG: Auction 59, lot 658 (cla). 34 Alamy Stock Photo: Science History Images (cla). Getty Images: Bettmann (br). Lawrence Berkeley National Laboratory: © 2010 The Regents of the University of California (cra). 35 Alamy Stock Photo: DPA Picture Alliance Archive (cr); Mieczyslaw Wieliczko (br). Getty Images: Bettmann (bc). Science Photo Library: Emilio Segre Visual Archives / American Institute of Physics (br). 36 Alamy Stock Photo: John Cancalosi (cra). Dorling Kindersley: Ruth

Jenkinson / RGB Research Limited (c, br). Science Photo Library. 37 Michael Brandon: (cra). Dorling Kindersley: Ruth Jenkinson / RGB Research Limited (tl, tr, br). Science Photo Library: PjrStudio (br). Dorling Kindersley: Ruth Jenkinson / RGB Research Limited (tc). Getty Images: Spaces Images (bl). Science Photo Library: Zephyr (ca). 39 Dorling Kindersley: Ruth Jenkinson / RGB Research Limited (cb, cr). Rex Shutterstock: Shutterstock / Mint Images (cla). Science Photo Library. 40 Alamy Stock Photo: John Cancalosi (ca). Science Photo Library: Public Health England (ca). 41 Alamy Stock Photo: Natural History Museum (tr); Science History Images (cla); Sciencephotos (br). Dorling Kindersley: Ruth Jenkinson / RGB Research Limited (bl). 42 Dorling Kindersley: Ruth Jenkinson / RGB Research Limited (tl). Science Photo Library: Ned Haines (cl). 42–43 Alamy Stock Photo: Science History Images. 43 123RF.com: Victor Bouchard (tc). Getty Images: Walter Bibikow (c); Scientifica (tr). Science Photo Library: Detlev van Ravenswaay (br). 44 Alamy Stock Photo: Ewing Galloway (cl); Keystone Pictures USA (br). US Department of Energy: (cl). 45 Alamy Stock Photo: Akademie (cra); Everett Collection Historical (tl); Heritage Image Partnership Ltd (bl); Science History Images (br). 46–47 123RF.com: Senohrabek (b). 46 Alamy Stock Photo: Phil Degginger (bl). Dorling Kindersley: Ruth Jenkinson / RGB Research Limited (cla, cl). 47 123RF.com: Fullempty (tr); Bogdan Ionescu (cla); Winterstorm (cr); Roman Samokhin (cb). Alamy Stock Photo: Simon Belcher (br). 48 Alamy Stock Photo: Nobeastsofierce (b). Dorling Kindersley: Ruth Jenkinson / RGB Research Limited (bl). Getty Images: John B. Carnett (c). 49 123RF.com: Ratchanida Thippayos (ca). Dorling Kindersley: Ruth Jenkinson / RGB Research Limited (bl, cr, tc). Getty Images: The Asahi Shimbun (br). 50 123RF.com: Oleksiy (cl). Dorling Kindersley: Ruth Jenkinson / RGB Research Limited (cb). Getty Images: Dimitri Otis (cl). Science Photo Library: James King-Holmes (br). 50–51 123RF.com: Aleksey Poprugin (cla); Anton Starikov (cb). Depositphotos Inc: Crstrbrt (tr). Getty Images: Hans-Peter Merten (tr). iStockphoto.com: Kerrick (tc). 52 Alamy Stock Photo: NPC Collection (cla); Sputnik (br); Traveler (tr). Dorling Kindersley: Ruth Jenkinson / RGB Research Limited (tc, cb). Rice University: Jeff Fitlow (bl). 53 123RF.com: James Blinn (br); mipan (bc). Dorling Kindersley: Ruth Jenkinson / RGB Research Limited (cl); Dave King / Durham University Oriental Museum (cb). 54 Dorling Kindersley: Ruth Jenkinson / RGB Research Limited (cla). 54–55 123RF.com: Ernie Janes (b). 55 123RF.com: Ayphoto (cra). Alamy Stock Photo: Robert Clayton (br). 56 Alamy Stock Photo: Science History Images (cr); Universal Images Group North America LLC / DeAgostini (cb). Dorling Kindersley: Ruth Jenkinson / RGB Research Limited (cla). Getty Images: Morley Read (bl). 57 123RF.com: Aleksandar Mijatovic (cb). Alamy

Stock Photo: Pictorial Press Ltd (cra). Dorling Kindersley: Ruth Jenkinson / RGB Research Limited (cla, bl). Getty Images: Universal History Archive (tl). 58 123RF.com: Wavebreak Media Ltd (crb). Dorling Kindersley: Ruth Jenkinson / RGB Research Limited (cl). Getty Images: Georgette Douwma (bl). 59 123RF.com: sin32 (br). Alamy Stock Photo: Falkensteinfoto (tr); Image Source (cb); The Granger Collection (tc). Getty Images: Harry Kikstra (tl). 60 Dorling Kindersley: Ruth Jenkinson / RGB Research Limited (cla, bl, cra). Jocelyn Rastel Lafond: (crb). Photo James D. Julia Auctioneers, Fairfield, Maine, USA www.jamesdjulia.com: Lamp by Charles Lotton "Multi Flora" 1993 (ca). 60–61 Getty Images: Barcroft Media / Massimo Rumi (b). 61 123RF.com: photo5963 (crb). Getty Images: Photofusion (cb). 62 Alamy Stock Photo: Brian Elliott (br). 63 123RF.com: Hieng Ling Tie (cra). Alamy Stock Photo: Paris Pierce (cl). Dorling Kindersley: Wardrobe Museum, Salisbury / Gary Ombler (bc). Getty Images: Andy Sotiriou (cr). 64 123RF.com: Sean Pavone (b). Alamy Stock Photo: I. Glory (cr). Dorling Kindersley: Ruth Jenkinson / RGB Research Limited (tr). Getty Images: Soltan Frédéric (c). 65 123RF.com: Sergey Mironov (cr). Dorling Kindersley: Ruth Jenkinson / RGB Research Limited (tc). Dreamstime.com: Daniel Poloha / Spidermont (cla). Getty Images: Keystone (bc). Science Photo Library: Union Carbide Corporation's Nuclear Division, courtesy Emilio Segre Visual Archives, Physics Today Collection / American Institute of Physics. 66–67 iStockphoto.com: (b). 66 Dorling Kindersley: Ruth Jenkinson / RGB Research Limited (cl). ESA: Hubble & NASA Processed by Judy Schmidt (bl). 67 123RF.com: (cl). Alamy Stock Photo: Keith Morris (cr). Dorling Kindersley: Ruth Jenkinson / RGB Research Limited (tl). 500px/ Henry Buchholtz (tr). 68 123RF.com: Scanrail (cla). Getty Images: Roger Bamber (br); ITAR-TASS Photo Agency (br). Dorling Kindersley: Ruth Jenkinson / RGB Research Limited (tl). Science Photo Library: Antonia Reeve (cra). 69 Alamy Stock Photo: Gordon Mills (bl); Prill Mediendesign (tl). Dorling Kindersley: Ruth Jenkinson / RGB Research Limited (tr, br). NASA: Christopher J. Lynch (Wyle Information Systems, LLC) (ca). Science Photo Library: Dirk Wiersma (cb). 70–71 123RF.com: Sean Pavone. Dorling Kindersley: Ruth Jenkinson / RGB Research Limited (c). 70 123RF.com: Ruslan Gilmanshin (b); Sandra van der Steen (ca). 71 © Rolls-Royce plc: (cr). US Department of Energy: (bc)

All other images © Dorling Kindersley

For further information see:
www.dkimages.com